DISCOVER

D0308386

1 Find a time when you can read the Bible each day

2 Find a place where you can be quiet and think

4 Ask God to help you understand what you read

3 Grab your Bible and a pencil or pen

5 Read today's Discover page and Bible bit

6 Pray about what you have read and learned

We want to...

- Explain the Bible clearly to you
- Help you enjoy your Bible
- Encourage you to turn to Jesus
- Help Christians follow Jesus

Discover stands for...

- Total commitment to God's Word, the Bible
- Total commitment to getting its message over to you

Team Discover

Martin Cole, Rachel Jones, Kirsty McAllister, Alison Mitchell, André Parker, Anne Woodcock, Ben Woodcraft
Discover is published by The Good Book Company, Blenheim House, 1 Blenheim Rd, Epsom, Surrey, KT19 9AP, UK.
Tel: 0333 123 0880; Email: discover@thegoodbook.co.uk UK: thegoodbook.co.uk
North America: thegoodbook.com   Australia: thegoodbook.com.au   NZ: thegoodbook.co.nz

How to use Discover

Here at Discover, we want you at home to get the most out of reading the Bible. It's how God speaks to us today. And He's got loads of top things to say.

We use the New International Version (NIV) of the Bible. You'll find that the NIV and New King James Version are best for doing the puzzles in Discover.

The Bible has 66 different books in it. So if the notes say...

Read Mark 6 v 1-3

...turn to the contents page of your Bible and look down the list of books to see what page Mark begins on. Turn to that page.

"Mark 6 v 1" means you need to go to chapter 6 of Mark, and then find verse 1 of chapter 6 (the verse numbers are the tiny ones). Then jump in and read it!

Here's some other stuff you might come across...

WEIRD WORDS

Felpagootle
These boxes explain baffling words or phrases we come across in the Bible.

Think!

This bit usually has a tricky personal question on what you've been reading about.

Action!

Challenges you to put what you've read into action.

Wow!

This section contains a gobsmacking fact that sums up what you've been reading about.

Pray!

Gives you ideas for prayer. Prayer is talking to God. Don't be embarrassed! You can pray in your head if you want to. God still hears you! Even if there isn't a Pray! symbol, it's a good idea to pray about what you've read anyway.

Coming up in Issue 2...

Mark: Who is Jesus?

We join Mark in the middle of his action-packed account of the life of Jesus. We see Jesus do and teach lots of amazing things that leave His friends, His enemies and even His own family baffled: just who *is* Jesus?!

Mark shows us that Jesus is the Messiah — the King God promised would rescue His people. It's great news! But Jesus also calls people to follow Him as their King. And that's definitely going to ruffle a few feathers...

Genesis: God's pomises

We jump into Genesis to meet Abram: an ordinary old man, who God makes extraordinary promises to!

Abram has no kids — but God promises to give him loads of descendants. Abram is living in a tent — but God promises to give his descendants a whole land of their own. Abram is nobody special — but God promises to bless the whole world through his family!

Watch as God follows through on His amazing promises, even when Abram tries to take matters into his own hands and messes up big time! See how God always keeps His promises, and is so loving and forgiving to those who trust Him.

Elisha: God's prophet

We turn to the book of 2 Kings to read about Elisha. He was a prophet, sent by God with a message for His people and their disobedient king! And to prove that Elisha really was His messenger, God did loads of astonishing miracles through him.

So brace yourself for bullying boys and man-eating bears, poison stew, floating axes and invisible fiery chariots. It all shows us God's great power, His love for His people, and how important it is for people to turn back and live His way.

Philippians: Joy for Jesus

The apostle Paul is writing a letter to his friends in Philippi... from prison. Does Paul's jail sentence get him down? No way! Because Paul is just so joyful about what God has done for him and for the Philippian Christians. He can't stop praising God!

Paul writes to the Philippian Christians to thank them for a gift they sent to him in prison. But he has loads more fantastic stuff to say about Jesus, and how to live for Him. He wants Christians to serve Jesus together as one united team!

Ready? Steady?
Let's go...

Mark: Who is Jesus?

In his book, Mark wants to show us who Jesus really is.

In the first five chapters, Mark has shown us that Jesus has power over nature, evil spirits, illness and even death.

WEIRD WORDS

Sabbath
Jewish holy day

Synagogue
Where people learned from Old Testament

Prophet
God's messenger

Jesus' amazing power points us to the fact that He is…

But today we'll meet some people who refused to believe that Jesus was God's Son.

Read Mark 6 v 1-3

Jesus was in Nazareth, the town where He'd grown up. So the people there knew lots about Him. They knew that…

Jesus was a

His mum was _ _ _ _

His brothers: _ _ _ _ _

_ _ _ _ **and**

They refused to believe that Jesus could be anyone special. They ignored all the signs.

Read verses 4-6

Jesus was amazed and saddened at their lack of faith (v6). They refused to see that God was working through Him. So Jesus did no more miracles in Nazareth. He gave them no more proof of who He was.

*Who do **you** think Jesus is?*

1) **A great teacher**
2) **Just an ordinary guy**
3) **A kind man**
4) **The Son of God**

Pray!

Dear God, help me not to ignore the amazing things I read about Jesus in Mark's book. Help me to believe that He really is God's Son.

A C D E F G H I J M N O P R S T U Y

2

**Mark
6 v 7-13**

Jesus has been travelling around, teaching and healing people.

Next, He sends out His disciples to do the same things.

WEIRD WORDS

Staff
Walking stick

Testimony
Evidence

Repent
Turn away from sin and start living for God

Anointed
Poured oil on their heads

Travelling light

All of today's missing words can be found in the wordsearch.

```
P  B  B  M  O  N  E  Y  X  C
Y  R  R  O  B  P  U  K  S  H
O  E  E  T  A  D  U  S  T  P
H  P  A  A  G  G  Q  N  A  G
S  E  D  L  C  Q  B  O  F  H
F  N  C  A  N  H  W  M  F  E
E  T  U  N  I  C  E  E  Z  A
E  X  T  R  A  E  F  D  E  L
T  R  I  H  S  S  H  A  K  E
S  A  N  D  A  L  S  R  L  D
```

Read Mark 6 v 7-10

What could they take?

S_____

S_____

What couldn't they take?

No b _____

No m_____

No e_____ s_____

They had to rely on God for everything. That's why they were not allowed to take money or extra stuff. Everywhere they went, God provided them with food, clothes and somewhere to stay!

Read verse 11

What should they do if they were not welcome in a town?

S_____ the d_____

from their f_____.

This showed that God isn't pleased with anyone who rejects His people or treats them badly.

Read verses 12-13

What else did the disciples do?

P_____ that

people should r_____,

drove out d_____ and

h_____ people.

There was nothing special about these disciples. But **Jesus** gave them the power to do these awesome things for Him!

Wow!

Do you sometimes feel unimportant or useless? God can use YOU to tell other people about Him! You just have to trust Him to help you.

Pray!

Ask God to help you to rely on Him for everything.
Ask Him to help you talk to people about Jesus.

3

Mark 6 v 14-29

Get ready to read a tragic story...

Dead wrong

Read Mark 6 v 14-16

Jesus was becoming famous because of His amazing miracles and great teaching. But people didn't realise He was God's Son.

Who did Herod think Jesus was?

**J_____ the B_____
raised from the d_____**

This was because he felt guilty for John's death.

Read verses 17-29

and number the story segments in the right order.

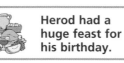
Herod had a huge feast for his birthday.

(1)

Herod arrested John when John told him he was disobeying God by marrying his brother's wife.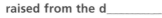

She asked for John to be beheaded.

So Herod had John executed. And John's followers buried him in a tomb.

Herod liked listening to John.

Herod's wife hated John.

Herod liked it and promised her anything she wanted.

His wife's daughter danced for him.

Later, when Herod heard about Jesus, he thought it must be John who'd come back from the dead! But he was dead wrong.

Wow!

Sadly, many people are still dead wrong about Jesus. They think He was just a good man or that He didn't even exist!

Pray!

Think of someone you know who doesn't understand who Jesus is. Ask God to help them see the truth about Jesus.

WEIRD WORDS

King Herod
Local ruler of Galilee

Elijah
Prophet who was around 800 years before Jesus

Prophet
God's messenger

Righteous and holy man
Someone who served God

Opportune
Perfect time

Oath
Special promise

Time with Jesus

The disciples (apostles) have just returned from their preaching and healing tour.

They've walked all the way, so they must be exhausted!

WEIRD WORDS

Apostles
Jesus would send out 11 of these men to tell people about Him

Solitary
Quiet, away from people

Compassion
Loving kindness

Read Mark 6 v 30-31

Jesus noticed they were tired.
What did He say to them?

a) This work is so important, there's no time to rest! ☐

b) Let's go somewhere quiet so you can rest for a while. ☐

c) You need a beach holiday in Greece. ☐

Jesus understood exactly how they were feeling. The best thing for them was to chill out—to have some time alone with Jesus.

Wow!

If life gets tough for you — family problems, friends hassling you, school getting too much for you...

Jesus understands exactly how you're feeling.

Action!

There's nothing better than to spend some time alone with Jesus, talking with Him. Do you set aside time each day to spend with Jesus? Why not set yourself a specific time?

Read verses 32-34

What happened?

a) They had a lovely rest ☐

b) They went windsurfing ☐

c) Loads of people got there before they did! ☐

What did Jesus do?

a) Told them to go away ☐

b) Had compassion for them and began teaching ☐

c) Hired windsurfers for everyone ☐

Jesus and His disciples didn't get much of a rest. But Jesus didn't get angry or turn the people away. Instead, He had compassion for them because He saw how much they needed Him.

Wow!

If you turn to Jesus because you need Him, He'll never be angry with you or turn you away. He longs to hear you.

Pray!

Will you tell Jesus what's on your mind right now?

Thousands of people followed Jesus and His disciples down to Lake Galilee.

Jesus was too loving to turn them away, so He spent ages teaching them.

Fishy feast

Read Mark 6 v 35-36

The disciples had to do some quick maths.

> 1000s of people
> + no food
> + a long way from the shops
> = A HUGE PROBLEM!

Actually, they did manage to find a tiny bit of food.

Read verses 37-38

What did they find?

> _____ loaves of bread
> + _____ fish

> 5 loaves
> + 2 fish
> = enough for a family picnic

but

> 5 loaves
> + 2 fish
> ÷ divided between 1000s
>   of people
> = NO CHANCE!

But all this doesn't add up to a problem for Jesus — God's Son!

Read verses 39-44

How many men ate? _____

Plus thousands of women and children too!

Because of His great love and compassion for these people, Jesus worked this incredible miracle. There were even 12 baskets of scraps left over!

Wow!

Nothing is impossible for God's Son! That means that even our biggest problems are no problem for Jesus.

Think!

What problems do you have?

_____

_____

_____

_____

_____

Pray!

Take your problems to Jesus right now and ask Him to help you with them.

6

*Jesus made
a meal for
thousands of
people from
only five loaves
of bread and
two fish!*

*It was a big sign
that He was
God's Son.*

Walking on water

Read Mark 6 v 45-46

What did Jesus do?

Went up a hill to p_____

Think!

Even though His life was hectic,
Jesus found time to talk to His
Father God. Do you make sure you
find time to spend alone talking
with God?

Read verses 47-52

and fill in the gaps.

**Late at night, the disciples
were in a b_____ on the
l_____. Jesus walked
on the w_____. The
disciples thought He was a
g_____ and were
t_____.
Jesus said "Don't be
a_____" and He
c_____ed into the boat.
The disciples were
completely a_____.**

The disciples hadn't understood
what had happened with the bread
and fish. That miracle was a big sign
that Jesus was **God's all-powerful
Son**. But they had missed the point.
That's why they were amazed when
Jesus walked on the water.

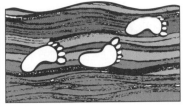

Think!

Do you believe that Jesus
is God's Son? That He has
power and authority over
everything?

Read verses 53-56

Jesus had become really famous.
Loads of people wanted to see His
miracles or be healed by Him. I
wonder if any of them realised that
these miracles were signs that Jesus
is **God's Son**?

Pray!

Mark wrote his book so readers
(like us!) would see who Jesus is
and trust in Him. If Mark's book
has shown you new things about
Jesus, spend time thanking God
right now.

For the free e-booklet
Why Did Jesus Come?, email
discover@thegoodbook.co.uk
or check out
www.thegoodbook.co.uk/contact-us
to find our UK mailing address.

7

**Mark
7 v 1-13**

Inside out

Mark wants to show us who Jesus really is. The disciples hadn't worked it out yet. And neither had the Pharisees…

Read Mark 7 v 1-5

Fill in the Pharisees' question.

> **Why don't your
> d_____ follow our
> tr_____ instead of
> eating their f_____ with
> un_____ hands?**

**Read verses 9-13
God says…**

HONOUR YOUR FATHER AND MOTHER

The Pharisees said…

> **But I've given all my
> money to the temple, so I
> don't have to look after my
> parents any more.**

Keeping these rules made them look godly, but inside they weren't really living for God at all!

Think!

Do you go to church, and try to appear godly and say the right things? But what about on the inside? Do you really live for God, or is it just a show?

WEIRD WORDS

Pharisees and teachers of the law
Jewish leaders. Most of them were against Jesus

Isaiah
A prophet, God's messenger

Prophesied
Predicted

Hypocrites
People who say one thing but do the opposite

Nullify
Cancel out. By obeying these rules, they had stopped obeying God's Word

The Jewish leaders had made loads of **rules** for the people to keep. One of these rules said that you must wash your hands in a special way before eating. If you didn't, then you weren't clean enough for God.

They thought that keeping these rules made them acceptable to God. But Jesus didn't agree…

Read verses 6-8

What did Isaiah say God thinks of people like this (v6)?

> **They h_____
> me with their _____
> but their h_____
> are far from me.**

Pray!

Ask God to help you to serve Him with your whole life. Not just on the outside. Not just on Sundays.

Clean sweep

**Mark
7 v 14-23**

The Pharisees thought that keeping rules (such as washing in a special way) made them clean and acceptable to God.

Read Mark 7 v 14-19

Jesus says it's not how we wash or what we eat that's important. He is much more bothered about sin — the things that really do make us unclean.

It's not what goes into someone that's the problem. It's what comes out. Wrong thoughts, words or actions.

Think!

What *unclean* stuff has come out of your mouth, mind, or actions recently? (Lies, swearing, cruel actions?)

_____

_____

_____

_____

_____

It's the sinful things which come out of us that God hates.

Read verses 20-23

Jesus lists some of the bad stuff that can come out of us. *Unjumble the anagrams to find them.*

E_____ T_____
LIVE   HOTTHUGS

T_____, M_____
FETHT   REDRUM

A_____
YULEDRAT

G_____, D_____
DERGE   ICE TED

S_____
DARNLES

F___ _____
LOLFY

This is the kind of stuff we need to fight against, because it offends God.

Pray!

If you really mean it, say sorry to God for the things you wrote under Think! Ask God to help you please Him more in what you think, say and do.

WEIRD WORDS

Parable
A story Jesus uses to explain a big truth

Dull
Stupid

Immorality
Sin

Adultery
Cheating on your husband or wife

Malice
Wanting to harm

Deceit
Lies, deceiving

Lewdness
Obscene, rude

Slander
Lying about someone

Folly
Foolishness

Gone to the dogs

Jesus has been teaching the crowds.

But now He moves on to a place called Tyre.

WEIRD WORDS

Vicinity
Surrounding area

Tyre
A Gentile (non-Jewish) city

Syrian Phoenicia
The country now known as Lebanon

Read Mark 7 v 24-26

History lesson

The Jews (called Israel in the Old Testament) were God's chosen people. God promised He would send a King to rescue them (Isaiah 9 v 6-7). This King was Jesus.

Many Jews believed that God had no time for Gentiles (non-Jews). So they treated people from other places badly—like this Greek woman who came to Jesus.

But God also promised that people from **all nations** (not just Israel) would have the chance to live with Him for ever! (Isaiah 66 v 18)

Read verse 27

Fill in the vowels (aeiou) to show what Jesus said to the woman.

> First let the ch__ldr__n eat all they w__nt. It's not r__ght to t__k__ the ch__ldr__n's br__ __d and toss it to the d__gs.

Jewish people were known as the "children of God". And they often called non-Jews "wild dogs".

Jesus was asking the woman if she really expected Him (a Jew) to help her (a Greek) when there were so many Jews that needed His help.

Read verses 28-30

What did she say to Jesus?

> L__rd, even the d__gs __nd__r the t__bl__ eat the ch__ldr__n's cr__mbs.

She **believed** that Jesus was the promised Jewish King. And she **believed** that He could help her, even though she wasn't Jewish (like a dog getting the crumbs of someone else's food). So Jesus healed her daughter!

Pray!

Jesus came for Jews **and** Gentiles. Thank God that Jesus came for **ANYONE** who believes He can rescue them from sin.

Right ear, right now

**Mark
7 v 31-37**

*Quick! Check
out what Isaiah
said about Jesus
hundreds of years
before Jesus was
born!*

*It's in Isaiah
35 v 5-6.*

WEIRD WORDS

Sidon
City not far from
Tyre

The Decapolis
An area of 10 cities,
south of Tyre, Sidon
and Galilee

> The blind will be able
> to see, and the deaf will
> hear! The lame will leap
> and dance, and those
> who can't speak will
> shout for joy!

Watch Isaiah's words come true!

Read Mark 7 v 31-35

and cross out the wrong words.

**Jesus left Wheel/Tyre/
Exhaust and went to the
Decapolis/Decathlon/
Decaffeinated. Some people
brought a man who was
dead/daft/deaf and could
hardly walk/squawk/talk.
Jesus put his fingers in the
man's ears/eyes/nose and
touched the man's tortoise/
tongue/tomato. Jesus looked
up to Hull/hell/heaven and
said *Ephphatha!/ Elephant!*
The man's ears were opened,
his tongue loosened and
he began to sneak/squeak/
speak.**

Read verses 36-37

Jesus had done an amazing thing.
But He told people to keep quiet
about it. He didn't want people
following Him just because they
thought He was a magician or a
great doctor. He wanted people to
realise that He was God's Son. But
most of them hadn't worked that
out yet.

Action!

Write down the names of people
you know who refuse to believe that
Jesus is God's Son.

_____

_____

_____

_____

Ask God to open their ears, so they
hear the truth about Jesus and start
living for Him.

More action!

Now write down the names of
Christians you know. Does that
include you?

_____

_____

_____

_____

Ask God to open their mouths so
they praise God loads and tell others
about Him!

Feeding time (again)

**Mark
8 v 1-10**

*Six days ago
we read about
Jesus feeding
thousands of
people with just
five loaves and
two fish.*

*Now He's about
to do something
very similar...*

WEIRD WORDS

Compassion
Loving kindness

Dalmanutha
Area near the Sea
of Galilee

Read Mark 8 v 1-10

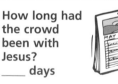

How long had
the crowd
been with
Jesus?
_____ days

The disciples
had only _____
loaves and a
few _____

How many
baskets did
they fill?
_____

How many
people did
Jesus feed?
_____

**But why did
Jesus do the same
miracle twice?**

**1. Jesus had c_____
for the people (v2)**

He cared for them and didn't want
them to go hungry. The brilliant
thing is that He cares for you and
me too!

Pray!

Thank Jesus that He is interested
in you and cares greatly for you!

**2. Because people had missed
the point**

They still hadn't worked out that
only **God's Son** could do these
awesome things.

Pray!

Ask God to help you understand
who Jesus is and what He's done
for you.

**3. Jesus was in the area of
the D_____
(Mark 7 v 31)**

That means there were loads of
Gentiles (non-Jews) in the crowd.
Last time, the crowd had been
mostly Jewish.

But Jesus' message was for
EVERYONE (not just Jews).

Pray!

Thank God that He sent
Jesus for **EVERYONE**.
Anyone at all can get to
know Jesus and have their lives
turned around by Him!

Read the signs

**Mark
8 v 11-13**

Read Mark 8 v 11-13

The Pharisees asked Jesus to give them a sign to prove that He was from God. UNBELIEVABLE!

Mark has told us about loads of amazing signs that Jesus gave. Draw lines to match the signs with the part of Mark they're in.

Jesus had been doing loads of amazing things.

Yet people still refused to see who He really is.

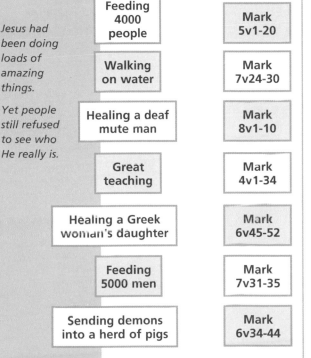

Feeding 4000 people	Mark 5v1-20
Walking on water	Mark 7v24-30
Healing a deaf mute man	Mark 8v1-10
Great teaching	Mark 4v1-34
Healing a Greek woman's daughter	Mark 6v45-52
Feeding 5000 men	Mark 7v31-35
Sending demons into a herd of pigs	Mark 6v34-44

Wow!

Look at the proof we've got…

- The Bible tells us all about Jesus' life.

- We can read prophecies about Jesus that came true (Isaiah 53 v 7, Mark 8 v 31).

- And what others said about Him (Paul in Romans 1 v 1-4).

- We're taught about Him in Christian meetings.

- He has changed the lives of Christians we know.

Think!

Do you still expect a special sign to prove that Jesus is God's Son? Or will you look at the evidence you already have?

The Pharisees had seen Jesus do amazing miracles, and they'd heard His wonderful teaching. Yet they still **refused to believe** that He was God's Son!

One more sign from Jesus wouldn't have changed their minds. They refused to believe, so Jesus wouldn't perform miracles just to please them.

WEIRD WORDS

Pharisees
Very strict
Jewish leaders

Pray! **Pick a prayer!**

a) Ask God to show you the truth about Jesus and help you understand who Jesus is.

b) Thank God for showing you that Jesus is His Son. Ask Him to help you explain to others who Jesus is.

13

**Mark
8 v 14-21**

Jesus has miraculously fed 4000 people from just a few loaves and fish.

Yet the Pharisees wouldn't believe that Jesus was God's Son!

Crazy!

WEIRD WORDS

Herod
Evil local ruler
(see Day 3)

Don't feast on yeast!

Read Mark 8 v 14-15

Go back one letter to reveal the weird thing that Jesus said.

— — — — —
X B U D I

— — —   — — —
P V U   G P S

— — —   — — — — —
U I F   Z F B T U

— —   — — —
P G   U I F

— — — — — — — —
Q I B S J T F F T

— — —   — —
B O E   P G

— — — —
I F S P E

Yeast facts!

When making bread, you put just a little bit of yeast in the mixture. But that little bit **spreads** throughout the whole loaf, helping it to rise.

Pharisee facts!

Jesus was warning His disciples about the Pharisees' wrong teaching and unbelief. It could **spread** a long way, just like yeast.

Read verses 16-21

Looks as if it has spread already! They thought He was talking about their sandwiches, but what did Jesus say?

— —   — — —
E P   Z P V

— — — — —   — — —
T U J M M   O P U

— — —   — —
T F F   P S

— — —   — — — —
B S F   Z P V S

— — — — — —
I F B S U T

— — — — — — — —?
I B S E F O F E

The disciples had seen Jesus do many amazing things, including feeding thousands of people from a tiny amount of food. And they'd heard His awesome teaching, yet they still didn't see that Jesus was God's Son!

Pray!

Tell God who YOU think Jesus is. Ask Him to help you see Jesus even more clearly as you read the Bible.

Genesis: God's promises

**Genesis
11 v 10-32**

Last issue, we began reading the action-packed book of Genesis.

Here's the story so far...

GENESIS UPDATE

- **God created the universe!**
- **Humans messed up God's perfect world by bringing sin into it.**
- **In fact, humans disobeyed God so much that He flooded the whole world.**
- **Only godly Noah and his family were saved.**

Now we pick up the story with Noah's son, Shem. Check out his family tree in **Genesis 11 v 10-26**.

Unjumble the anagrams to reveal the names.

A_____
       D A H A R P A X

E_____
       B E E R

R_____
       U R E

S_____
       H E L A S H

S_____
       R U G E S

P_____
       G L E E P

N_____
       R O H A N

T_____
       H E A R T

Read verses 27-32

Finally we get to meet **A**_____
                    RAMBA

and his wife **S**_____
              A R I A S

and his nephew **L**_____
               T O L

We'll be reading loads about this family, and God's special relationship with Abram.

Remember that fact; it will be important later. God was going to do amazing things, starting with this little family.

> **What was sad about Sarai (v30)?**

WEIRD WORDS

Conceive
Have children

Pray!

Thank God that He can use anyone in His great plans. Ask Him to teach you loads as you read Genesis.

15

**Genesis
12 v 1-9**

It's time to meet Abram.

As we'll see, God made some amazing promises to him.

WEIRD WORDS

Accumulated
Gained over the years

Offspring
Children and descendants

Altar
A special table. On it, God's people cooked special animals and gave them (as a sacrifice) to God

Get up and go

Read Genesis 12 v 1-3

and decode God's promises.

PROMISE 1

God promised that Abram's family would grow into a great nation (v2). But Abram was 75 and his wife Sarai was not able to have children. Impossible, surely?

PROMISE 2

Through Abram, God would bless the whole world (v3). Jesus would be a descendant of Abram. God blessed (showed His care for) the world by sending Jesus into it.

Read verses 4-5

God told Abram to leave his own country and his father's family, and go to a strange new land (v1). It was a step into the unknown, but Abram trusted God to look after him, and set off on the long journey.

Read verses 6-9

PROMISE 3

God promised to give this whole country to Abraham's descendants! (v7) This promise looked unlikely too, but one day God would use Joshua to lead His people into the land.

Pray!

Abram left everything behind to obey God and go to this strange new land. Ask God to help you to trust and obey Him as much as Abram did.

A	B	C	D	E	G	H	I	L	N	R	S

**Genesis
12 v 10-20**

*Things are going
well for Abram.*

*God has made
three fantastic
promises to him
(see yesterday's
Discover).*

*And Abram
has shown he
trusts God by
obeying Him and
travelling to a
new country.*

WEIRD WORDS

Famine
Not enough food

Pharaoh
King of Egypt

Inflicted
Sent as a
punishment

Pharaoh tale

*That's like a fairy tale but, er,
a bit Egyptian!*

Everything would be fine as long as
Abram kept trusting God…

Oh dear.

*How many times do the words **God**
or the **Lord** appear in verses 10-20?*

_____

Not enough. God's not mentioned
much because Abram didn't turn to
God for help. He stopped trusting
God and ended up in a heap of
trouble.

Wow!

It's always a mistake to
tackle a problem without
asking God for help.

Read Genesis 12 v 10-16

*Did Abram ask God to keep him and
Sarai safe from Pharaoh?*

YES/NO _____

Abram ended up lying to keep
himself safe. And Pharaoh took
Sarai to live with him in his palace
because he thought she wasn't
married. What a mess!

Wow!

Ignoring God and taking
things into our own hands
often messes things up.
We can end up doing wrong, just as
Abram did.

Read verses 17-20

Did the Lord forget Abram?

YES/NO _____

Did He rescue Abram and Sarai?

YES/NO _____

Although Abram ignored Him,
the Lord still rescued Abram from
Pharaoh!

Action!

We get into all kinds of trouble
when we try to live our lives
without God.

When life seems difficult and
you're feeling low, TURN TO GOD
and trust Him to help you.

Lots of land for Lot

Genesis 13 v 1-13

Abram and his nephew Lot are now really rich!

So what's their problem?

WEIRD WORDS

The Negev
Desert area

Livestock
Farm animals, like sheep, goats and cows

Herdsmen
Men who looked after the animals

Plain
Large, flat area of land

Jordan
Huge river

Read Genesis 13 v 1-7

Abram and Lot had loads and loads of sheep, goats and cattle. But there wasn't enough water or grass to feed them all. This led to arguments between Abram's herdsmen and Lot's herdsmen.

Read verses 8-9

What did Abram say (v9)?

Let's _____.

If you go _____

I'll go _____.

Abram suggested they split up to avoid any more quarrels. He had the right to choose who farmed where because he was top man in the family. But he let Lot choose instead. Generous.

Action!

How can you be more generous, like Abram?

Maybe letting your friends choose what to do, rather than getting your own way?

Or being nice to your sister to avoid a big argument?

_____
_____
_____
_____

Read verses 10-13

Check out Lot's choice:

A The beautiful plain of Jordan. Plenty of grass and water for his animals. But close to the evil city of Sodom.	**B** The hills of Canaan. Harder to farm, but well away from Sodom and the sinful people who lived there.

Did Lot choose A or B (v11)? ☐

Later on, we'll see what a bad decision it was to move near to such sinful people.

We often have **tough choices** to make. Like whether or not to hang out with certain friends we like, even though they get up to stuff we know is wrong.

Pray!

Ask God to help you make wise choices, especially about the people you hang out with. And ask Him to help you do the stuff you wrote under "action".

18

**Genesis
13 v 14-18**

Abram and Lot had so many animals that they had to split up and move to different areas.

Lot got quality land near the River Jordan, and Abram was left with the not-so-nice hill country.

WEIRD WORDS

Offspring
Children and descendants

Length and breadth
All of the land

Showing promise

It looked as though Abram had lost out, but God had great news for him…

Read Genesis 13 v 14-15

God told Abram to look all around him — north, east, south and west. *What was God's great promise to Abram? Go back one letter to find out (B=A, C=B, D=C).*

‾B‾M‾M   ‾U‾I‾E

‾M‾B‾O‾E   ‾U‾I‾B‾U

‾Z‾P‾V   ‾T‾F‾F   ‾J

‾X‾J‾M‾M   ‾H‾J‾W‾F

‾U‾P   ‾Z‾P‾V

‾B‾O‾E   ‾Z‾P‾V‾T

‾P‾G‾G‾T‾Q‾S‾J‾O‾H

And that's not all…
Read verses 16-18

‾J   ‾X‾J‾M‾M

‾N‾B‾L‾F   ‾Z‾P‾V‾S

‾P‾G‾G‾T‾Q‾S‾J‾O‾H

‾M‾J‾L‾F   ‾U‾I‾F

‾E‾V‾U‾U   ‾P‾G

‾U‾I‾F   ‾F‾B‾S‾U‾I

God promised Abram that his family would be so large it would be as hard to count as all the dust in the world! And God would give them all this land too!

Wow!

God has made amazing promises to all of His people. Check out these two…

Jeremiah 29 v 11-14
John 3 v 16-18

Action!

Pick one of the verses from those Bible bits and turn it into a poster.

Pray!

Thank the Lord for His awesome promises to His people!

Lot of trouble

*Amraphel!
Kedorlaomer!
Shemeber!*

*Today we're
going to read
about some
bizarrely named
kings having a big
fight!*

WEIRD WORDS

Subject to
Ruled by

Allied with
On the same side

Hebrew
Hebrews would be
God's chosen people

Routed
Defeated

Don't be put off by all the weird
names in today's reading.

Stick with it and you'll see that what
happened was that **4 powerful
kings** attacked the **5 cities** on the
plain of Jordan (including evil city
Sodom).

Read Genesis 14 v 1-12

Last time we read about Lot, he was
living *near* Sodom.

But now it seems he's chosen to
move into that evil city!

Think!

What places is it best not
to hang around? And who
is it best not to get too friendly with,
in case you're tempted to join in with
what they do?

Lot and his family were kidnapped,
and all his possessions were stolen.
It's time for Abram to come to the
rescue…

Read verses 13-16

*Fill in the gaps to complete the
description of Abram's rescue.*

**1. Abram got his friends
M_____, E_____
and A_____ to help him
out (v13).**

**2. He grabbed the _____
men who worked for him
and chased the 4 kings as far
as D_____ (v14).**

**3. Abram d_____
his men into groups, then
attacked the enemy and
defeated them! (v15)**

**4. Abram r_____ed
all the stuff that had been
stolen. He also brought back
L_____ and the w_____
and other p_____ (v16)**

Abram's plan worked perfectly and
Lot was saved. *But who was really
behind this rescue? The answer is in
verse 20*.

Pray!

Thank God that nothing is too
difficult for Him.
If anything is bothering you right
now, tell God about it.
He can help you!

Meet Mel

**Genesis
14 v 17-24**

God helped
Abram to defeat
the armies of four
powerful kings.
And to rescue
Lot, the people
of Sodom, and all
their possessions.

WEIRD WORDS

Oath
Promise

Read Genesis 14 v 17-18

*Fill in the vowels to show who came
out to meet Abram.*

The k__ng of S__d__m and M__lch__z__d__k, k__ng of S__l__m

*What was unusual about this
Melchizedek guy?*

He was a pr__ __st as well as a k__ng

Priest and King

The book of Hebrews tells us that
Melchizedek reminds us of **Jesus**.
Jesus is also a King and a Priest, but
far greater.

Jesus is King over everything. And
He is the ultimate Priest because,
when He died and rose again, He
took away the sins of God's people.
(It's all in Hebrews 7 v 23-28.)

Read verses 18-20

Melchizedek praised God for giving
Abram a great victory over the four
kings.

Action!

On spare paper, write
down some of the things
you can praise and thank
God for. Put SENDING JESUS at the
top of the list!

priest   king   Jesus

Read verses 21-24

Usually the reward for winning a
battle was to keep everything (and
everyone) you captured.

But Abram refused to keep any of
the things the king of Sodom gave
him. He wanted people to know
that everything he had came from
God. And he gave a tenth of his
possessions back to God too (v20).

Think!

Everything you have
comes from God. What
can you give back to Him?
Money? Time?

_____

_____

_____

_____

Pray!

Thank God that everything you
have comes from Him. Spend
time praising Him for the things
you wrote down earlier.

Stars in his eyes

Genesis
15 v 1-6

gnirpsffo   dleihs

deveileb   diarfa

srats   yks

drawer   tnuoC

Today's missing words can be found written backwards in the word pool.

Read Genesis 15 v 1

What encouraging words did God have for Abram?

Don't be a_____ Abram. I am your s_____ and your great r_____.

C_____ the stars.

You will have as many

o_____ as the

s_____ in the s_____!

Read verse 6

Abram

b_____ God

Abram wasn't perfect. He'd let God down in the past. But because Abram trusted God, the Lord accepted him. In God's eyes, it was as if Abram had never done anything wrong.

Wow!

God was Abram's King and would protect him. He'd already proved this by helping Abram defeat the four kings.

And even though Abram was rich, his greatest reward was having God as his friend! And that's true for all of God's people (Christians).

Read verses 2-5

Despite God's encouragement, Abram was still fed up because he had no children. No one to continue the family and inherit everything of Abram's. But God had promised to give Abram children. And He now repeated that promise (v5).

WEIRD WORDS

Sovereign
In control of everything

Estate
Wealth, land and possessions

Heir
The person who'll inherit someone's estate

Credited (to him as...)
Given, not earned

Righteousness
Being right with God — forgiven by Him

Wow!

We can trust God's promises too. If we trust His promise to forgive us (because of Jesus' death in our place), then God accepts us too. He will forgive us for all the wrong stuff we've done!

A game of 2 halves

**Genesis
15 v 7-21**

*God promised
to give the
whole land
of Canaan
to Abram's
descendants.*

WEIRD WORDS

**Ur of the
Chaldeans**
Where Abram's
family was from

Heifer
Young cow

Carcasses
Dead bodies

Amorites
The sinful people
who lived in Canaan

Brazier
Pot of hot coals

Covenant
Agreement

But Abram wanted proof that God would keep His promise.

Read Genesis 15 v 7-11

A **covenant** was an agreement that shouldn't be broken. To show He would keep His promises, God was going to make a covenant with Abram.

So why all the dead animals?

When people made covenants, they killed some animals or birds, then walked through the dead bodies.

If you broke the agreement, you'd be cut to pieces like the animals!

Read verses 12-16

God told Abram what would happen to his family (the Israelites) in the future. *Match up each promise with what actually happened.*

Your family will be slaves in another country for 400 years (v13)	**God rescued them and punished the Egyptians (Exodus 14 v 26-31)**
I will rescue your family and punish their enemies (v14)	**God took the Israelites into Canaan (Joshua 1 v 1-5)**
You, Abram, will die peacefully at a good old age (v15)	**Exodus 12 v 40**
Your descendants will return here to live in Canaan (v16)	**Genesis 25 v 7-8**

All of the things God promised Abram came true! He really does keep His promises!

Read verses 17-21

The pot of fire and burning torch were a sign of God's presence. God Himself passed between the animal bodies to show that He really would keep His promises.

Pray!

"Thank You, Lord, that You always keep Your promises. Help me to trust You more and remember all that You've done for me."

You've got Ishmael

Genesis 16 v 1-16

How good are you at waiting? Are you really patient, or does it wind you up to wait for stuff?

Fill in the Os, Es and Ss to reveal one of God's promises to Abram.

I will mak___ y___ur ___ff___pring lik___ th___ du___t ___f th___ ___arth (Genesis 13 v 16)

God had promised to give them children, but Abram and Sarai wouldn't wait for God…

Read Genesis 16 v 1-6

They had waited for 10 years for God to give them a son, but eventually they gave up on God and tried to fix the problem themselves. Look at all the trouble this caused…

• Hagar b___cam___ pr___gnant and b___gan t___ hat___ ___arai.

• ___arai blam___d Abram.

• ___arai tr___at___d Hagar badly until ___he ran away from home.

Wow!

Sometimes it's hard to trust that God will do what's best for us. Instead of turning to Him in prayer and waiting for His answer, we try to sort it out on our own. But God's way is always the best way.

Read verses 7-16 *and complete the story.*

Hagar fl___d t___ th___ d___ ___ ___rt. Th___ ang___l ___f th___ L___rd f___und Hagar and t___ld h___r t___ r___turn t___ ___arai. H___ pr___mi___ ___d that sh___ w___uld hav___ l___ts ___f d___ ___c___ndants.

What else did the angel say?

Y___u will hav___ a s___n and nam___ him I___hma___l, f___r th___ L___rd ha___ h___ard y___ur mi___ ___ry.

God showed His great love to Hagar. But Ishmael wasn't the son God had promised Abram. They'd have to wait a bit longer.

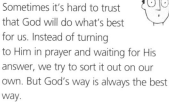

Pray!

Ask God to help you trust Him more. And to give you the patience to wait for His help.

WEIRD WORDS

Conceived
Became pregnant

Submit to her
Obey her

Ishmael
Means *God hears*

Wild donkey
He would live alone like a wild desert donkey

Hostility
Anger, hatred

Beer Lahai Roi
Means *Well of the Living One who sees me*

24

Lifetime guarantee

Genesis 17 v 1-14

Abram hadn't trusted God to give him a son.

But God would still keep His promise to Abram...

WEIRD WORDS

Blameless
Godly. Not perfect, but living God's way

Covenant
God's great promises to Abram (see Genesis 12 v 1-3)

Fruitful
Have lots of children

Read Genesis 17 v 1-2

God told Abram to keep obeying Him and living for Him.

Think!

It's one thing *saying* that we trust God and live for Him, but we've got to actually do it! What can you change in your life so you serve God more?

Read verses 3-5

What did God change Abram's name to?

[   ]

That means **father of many**. God would keep His promise to give Abraham loads of descendants.

Read verses 6-8

Every time God mentioned His covenant promise, Abraham learned a bit more about what was in store for him and his descendants.

Whole n_____ would be descended from Abraham (v6).

And some of his family would be k_____! (v6)

God promised to be the God of Abraham's d_____ too (v7).

And God's promise of a land to live in is e_____ (v8). Even when this world is no more, God's people will live with Him for ever!

Read verses 9-14

Weird. Every male in Abraham's family had to be circumcised. That meant having part of the skin around the penis cut off. Ouch!

This would be a sign of God's covenant promises to them. A sign that they were God's people.

Pray!

Read verse 1 again. Ask God to help you to walk His way and live for Him.

Promise keeper

God is still talking to Abraham, and making even more amazing promises.

Read Genesis 17 v 15-22

```
SIMSASYARHCRAMOAHAV
HWEEWILNILWALLINLBL
THELWATFIVHALEETLAM
HBSOEEOTRWNHTICEWTA
REHLOLILFVSENEADARA
ITUCSILTAOEOANROCSS
```

To find one of God's promises, take **every 4th letter** in the grid, starting with the **1st S**.

1. S_____

_____

_____ (v16)

This promise came true. Abraham and Sarah had many descendants, turning into whole nations. Some of them were kings, like David.

Now take every **4th letter**, starting with the **2nd S**.

2. S_____

_____

_____ (v19)

God promised that Sarah would give birth to a son, within one year (v21). Even though she was 90! God kept this promise too **(Gen 21 v 1-3)**.

Take every **4th letter**, starting with the **1st M**.

3. M_____

_____

_____ (v21)

God would have a covenant with Isaac too. His many descendants would live in Canaan. And the whole world would be blessed through a member of his family: Jesus.

Now take **every 4th letter**, starting with the **1st I**.

4. I_____

_____

_____ (v20)

Genesis 25 v 12-18 tells us how this promise came true too.

All of this is even more proof that God always keeps His promises!

Read verses 23-27

Yesterday we read how God told Abraham to circumcise all the males in his family. It was a sign of God's covenant with Abraham's family. Abraham obeyed God.

Wow!

Don't worry, we don't have to be circumcised these days! But we can show God that we trust Him by obeying His word, the Bible.

More about Abraham in a few weeks…

Elisha: God's prophet

**2 Kings
2 v 19-22**

Did you get **Elijah?** We read about him in Issue One of Discover.

Elijah was God's prophet: he spoke God's words to the Israelites, telling them to turn away from false gods and turn back to God.

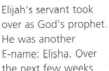

Amazingly, Elijah didn't die. God took Elijah straight up to heaven in a chariot and a whirlwind!

Elijah's servant took over as God's prophet. He was another E-name: Elisha. Over the next few weeks we'll read how God used Elisha to do amazing things.

Read 2 Kings 2 v 19-22

and fill in the gaps.

Some men from Jericho told Elisha that the w_____ was b_____ and the land couldn't produce enough crops for food (v19).

Bizarrely, Elisha said, *"Bring me a new b_____ and put s_____ in it"* (v20).

Elisha threw the s_____ into a s_____ and the Lord h_____ the water! (v21-22)

The Israelites had repeatedly turned away from God and worshipped fake gods. God owed them nothing. In fact, they deserved His punishment.

Yet God healed their water so that their crops could grow again. What an amazing, loving, forgiving God!

Pray!

Thank God for His incredible love and kindness. Thank Him for specific things in your life. Family, friends, answers to prayer, etc. And ask Him to teach you loads as you read about Elisha in 2 Kings.

OK, brainiac...

How many Bible characters can you name, beginning with the letter E?

E_____

E_____

E_____

E_____

E_____

E_____

E_____

E_____

Eutychus Elihu
Eliphaz Ephraim
Elkanah Elizabeth
Eleazar Eli Elimelech
Ezra Esther Ezekiel
Eglon Elijah Elisha
Eve Esau Enoch Ehud

Get any of these?

The bear facts

**2 Kings
2 v 23-25**

Do you like strange stories?

Well, today's is as strange as they get.

It involves a bald man, some bad boys and 2 bears!

Read 2 Kings 2 v 23-25.

Then fill in the missing letters.

As Elisha was walk__ng alo__g t__e road, some boys cam__ out of the tow__ and jeered __t hi__. "G__t out of here, baldy!" they said. "Get __ut of here, baldy!" He __urned round, looked at t__em and called a curs__ on them in the name of the __ord. Then tw__ bea__s came out of the woods and maule__ forty two of the boys.

What a weird story! It seems a huge over-reaction from Elisha. To set two bears on them just because they called him a baldy!

Below, write out the letters you just filled in. In the same order.

Elisha cursed them

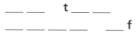

__ __   t __ __

__ __ __ __   __ f

__ __ __   __ __ __ __

Elisha was God's messenger, and spoke on God's behalf.

So did Elisha go over the top? Let's look at the facts…

1. This large group of boys jeered at Elisha probably because he was God's prophet and they worshipped false gods.

2. Mocking God's messenger is like mocking God Himself.

3. So God sent the bears to maul them. It was the punishment they deserved.

4. God is always fair.

Elisha did the right thing.
The boys were rightly punished for mocking God.

Think!

Who teaches you God's Word, the Bible?

_____

_____

_____

Do you ever mock them or disrupt what they're doing? You probably won't be eaten by a bear! But it's a seriously bad thing to do.

Pray!

Say sorry to God for times when you've mocked Him or His servants. Pray for the people you wrote down. Ask God to help and encourage them as they teach His Word.

**2 Kings
3 v 1-8**

Today in 2 Kings we're going to read about 3 kings...

We 3 kings...

Read 2 Kings 3 v 1-3

HISTORY FILE

- **God's people, the Israelites, had split into 2 kingdoms.**

- **The northern kingdom was called *Israel*. It was ruled by *King Joram*. He was evil and disobeyed God.**

- **The southern kingdom was called *Judah*. It was ruled by *King Jehoshaphat*. He served God.**

And here comes a third king...

Read verses 4-5

 The country of Moab was ruled by Israel. So the Moabites had to give Israel 100,000 lambs and loads of wool every year! But Mesha, the king of Moab, was sick of this and attacked Israel.

King Joram of Israel needed help to fight the Moabites, so he asked Jehoshaphat. But Joram hated God and Jehoshaphat loved God. Surely Jehoshaphat wouldn't team up with evil Joram!

Read verses 6-8

and fill in Jehoshaphat's reply (v7) in your own words.

Will you fight with me against King Mesha?

Jehoshaphat said there was no difference between them!

Christians sometimes...

- pretend they are no different

- hang out with people who are a bad influence on them

- make decisions without asking God first

Think!

Do you do any of those things? Sometimes we can leave God out of our everyday lives.

Pray!

Ask God to help you please Him in the way you act with your friends. And to serve Him in your everyday life.

Thirsty work

2 Kings
3 v 9-12

Battle latest...

Godly King Jehoshaphat has joined forces with evil King Joram.

They're marching their large army through the desert of Edom, to fight the Moabites.

WEIRD WORDS

King of Edom
Local leader who was ruled by King Jehoshaphat

Enquire
Ask

Pour water
He was Elijah's assistant

Read 2 Kings 3 v 9

Uh-oh. After 7 days of marching, what disaster struck? *Go back one letter to work it out.*

___ ___ ___ ___   ___ ___ ___
U I F Z   S B O

___ ___ ___   ___ ___
P V U   P G

___ ___ ___ ___ ___
X B U F S

The two kings reacted very differently to this tricky situation.

Read verse 10

What did Joram (the king of Israel) say?

___ ___ ___   ___ ___ ___
I B T   H P E

___ ___ ___ ___ ___
I B O E F E

___ ___   ___ ___ ___ ___
V T   P W F S

___ ___   ___ ___ ___ ___?
U P   N P B C

Joram did not serve God, so he didn't trust God to help them.

Read verses 11-12

What did Jehoshaphat say?

___ ___   ___ ___ ___ ___ ___
J T   U I F S F

___   ___ ___ ___ ___ ___ ___ ___
B   Q S P Q I F U

___ ___ ___ ___   ___ ___
I F S F   X F

___ ___ ___   ___ ___ ___?
D B O   B T L

Prophets were God's messengers. They told people what God wanted to say to them. Jehoshaphat wanted to visit Elisha and find out what God wanted them to do.

Think!

Imagine you're in a tricky situation. Maybe trouble at school. Or a family problem. How do you react?

a) Like Joram, blaming God? Or not even thinking about God at all?

b) Like Jehoshaphat, turning to God for help?

Pray!

Talk to God about what's going on in your life right now. Ask Him to help you out, and to help you rely on Him more.

Thirst quencher

**2 Kings
3 v 13-20**

The story so far:

*Godly King
Jehoshaphat
and evil King
Joram have
joined forces
against the
Moabites.*

*But they've
run out of
water and have
turned to God's
prophet, Elisha,
for help.*

WEIRD WORDS

Harpist
Played soothing
harp music to relax
Elisha

Sacrifice
Gift to God

What would you say if the Queen of
England asked you for a favour?

> **Shove off!
> We've got nothing
> in common with
> each other!**

You probably wouldn't talk to her
like that, would you?!!

But that's just how Elisha spoke to
the king of Israel.

Read 2 Kings 3 v 13-15

Joram hated God, just as his parents
(Ahab and Jezebel) had. No wonder
God and His prophet refused to
answer Joram.

*Use the numbers under the letters
to unscramble the code.*

GOD WOULD
23 8 3   6 8 5 22 3

NOT ANSWER
21 8 16   12 21 9 6 20 10

— — — — —
18 8 10 12 1

JUST LOOK
18 5 9 16   22 8 8 7

AT VERSE 14
12 16   15 20 10 9 20

WHY DID GOD
6 4 17   3 19 3   23 8 3

HELP THEM?
4 20 22 2   16 4 20 1

F __ __   __ __ __
  8 10   16 4 20

__ __ __   __ F
9 12 7 20 8

__ __ __ __ __ __ __ __ __ __ __
18 20 4 8 9 4 12 2 4 12 16

God answered His servant
Jehoshaphat.

Read verses 16-20

Jehoshaphat loved God and trusted
Him. God not only gave them water
from nowhere, but He also promised
to give them victory against Moab!

Pray!

Thank God that He's so good to
His people (Christians), and that
He gives them far more than they
ask for or deserve.

Massacre in Moab

31

**2 Kings
3 v 21-27**

*Yesterday we
saw how God
answered
Jehoshaphat's
cry for help, and
provided water
from out of
nowhere!*

WEIRD WORDS

Bear arms
It means to carry
weapons, not to
wear t-shirts!

The plunder
Anything they
could steal from the
Israelite camp

Kir Hareseth
The capital city of
Moab

Fury
Moab's anger
against the Israelites

But God didn't stop there.

*Look again at **2 Kings 3 v 18**. The
second half of the verse says:*

He will also

_____

_____

_____

Moab was the country that Kings
Jehoshaphat and Joram were
fighting against.

Now read verses 21-27

God gave Jehoshaphat much more
than just the water he asked for.
God gave him a great victory too.
What a great God!

He deserves all the praise we can
give Him!
*Check out how Paul praises God in
Ephesians 3 v 20-21.*

Action!

When God answers
your prayers (maybe
in a more amazing way than you'd
ever imagined!), thank and praise
Him! In fact, spend some time
praising God right now…

You might find it helpful to grab
some paper and write out Ephesians
3 v 20-21 in your own words.

After God had given the Israelites
victory, they didn't forget to do
what He'd told them to (check out
v19 and v25).

**It wasn't just a nasty piece
of vandalism! There was
a good reason for God
telling them to ruin the
fields and block up the
wells. It would take the
Moabites a long time to
get their country back
to normal. And they
definitely wouldn't argue
with the God of Israel and
Judah for a long time!**

Verse 27 tells us that the king of
Moab disgustingly sacrificed his own
son to a fake god. After that, for
some reason, the Israelites stopped
their attack. They didn't finish off
God's job.

Pray!

What commands do you find hard
to keep? Obeying your parents?
Not stealing? Ask God to help
you to obey Him even when it's
really hard.

32

Q. What do
   you get if
   you cross a
   widow, a pot
   of oil, and a
   prophet?

A. An amazing
   miracle!

WEIRD WORDS

Company of the prophets
Group of men who served God

Revered
Loved and respected

Creditor
Person he owed money to

Oil
Olive oil for cooking

Man of God
Elisha

One for oil and oil for one

Read 2 Kings 4 v 1

This woman was in loads of trouble. She couldn't pay off her husband's debts, and no one else would. It looked as though she would lose both of her sons!

Take every 2nd letter (starting with L) to reveal what James 1v27 says.

N W G I L D O O O W K S A I F N T T E H R E O I R R S P R S H U A H F N S E A R N I D N

L_ _ _ _

_ _ _ _ _ _

_ _ _ _ _ _ _

_ _ _

_ _ _ _ _ _

_ _   _ _ _ _ _ _ _

_ _ _ _ _ _ _ _ -

_ _ _ _

Action!

God cares for those who no one else cares for. We can follow His example. Maybe by befriending an old lady who has no family. Or regularly giving money or time to a charity that cares for people.

What could you do?

_____

_____

_____

Tearfund is a Christian charity that helps people without food, money or homes. Their website is www.tearfund.org

Back to the story! The woman went to God's prophet Elisha for help…

Read verses 2-7

That's amazing! This woman was in real trouble. She turned to God for help, by visiting Elisha the prophet. He told her to pour oil into pots and she trusted God to fill them. And God did!

Think!

We can turn to God and tell Him our troubles. He will answer our prayers. Not always immediately, or in the way we expect, but He does answer! Do you trust Him to help you?

Wow!

Our biggest problem is SIN — it's like a huge debt we can't pay. But if we trust Jesus, He will pay the debt for us, so we can have eternal life in heaven.

Gifts from God

**2 Kings
4 v 8-17**

Elisha didn't have his own room because he travelled about so much.

But that was about to change when he met someone else who loved God.

Read 2 Kings 4 v 8-10

How did this woman show her love for God?

> **By being kind to**
>
> _____

She gave him a meal every time he passed through the area.

Then she built an extension on her house for Elisha to stay in!

Read verses 11-16

In those days it was considered a bad thing to have no children. No one to carry on the family name. No one to look after her when she grew old. No one to inherit the family's land and possessions.

Fill in the vowels (aeiou).

**About th__s t__m__
n__xt y__ __r,
you will h__ld a
s__n in y__ __r __rms!**

Don't mislead your s___rv___nt!

The woman didn't want to get her hopes up. But Elisha was serious about thanking this woman, and he knew that God could give her a baby.

Write down 3 people who do a lot for you…

_____

_____

_____

Now write down 3 things you can do to say thank you…

_____

_____

_____

Now make sure you do them!

Read verse 17

Pray!

Wow. God is so good to His people! What can you thank Him for right now?

A very sad day

2 Kings
4 v 18-31

Remember the woman who built a room for Elisha?

WEIRD WORDS

Reapers
Crop gatherers

Man of God
Elisha

New Moon or Sabbath
Special days for Jewish people

Staff
Walking stick

Rejoice
Celebrate!

Grief
Sadness

Trials
Tough times

Salvation
Rescue

God gave her and her husband a surprise present — a baby! But that's not the end of the story…

Read 2 Kings 4 v 18-23

She must have been so upset, but she didn't blame God. Instead, she went as fast as she could to Elisha, God's prophet.

Think!

When things go wrong, is your first reaction to ask God to help you? Or do you blame Him for what's happened?

Read verses 24-26

What surprising thing did she say? Cross out the all Cs to find out.

```
CEVCERCCYCTHICNGC
CICCSALCLRICGCHTCC
```

E_____
_____!

Didn't she care?

Read verse 27-28

Of course she cared! She was hugely upset and couldn't understand what God was doing. But she still turned to God (and His prophet Elisha) for help and comfort. That's a great example for us to follow.

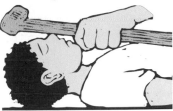

Read verses 29-31

Gehazi couldn't heal the boy.

Check out 1 Peter 1 v 6-9

Peter says that Christians go through tough times. It's all part of God's plans. When we come through tough times, it strengthens our trust in God. And brings glory to Him.

It can be really hard to keep going as a Christian. But even when we can't understand what God is doing, Christians can still be happy that Jesus has saved them from sin.

And one day they'll go to live with Him for ever!

Pray!

Tell God what's worrying you at the moment (however big or small it seems!). Ask for help to keep trusting Him and to not give up.

For a free fact sheet about *Facing Tough Times*, email discover@thegoodbook.co.uk or check out www.thegoodbook.co.uk/contact-us to find our UK mailing address.

Don't worry, it's not over yet! More tomorrow…

Wakey wakey!

**2 Kings
4 v 32-37**

Back to the sad story of the woman from Shunem and her dead son...

What do you mean "back to the story"? The boy's dead, the story's over!

Not quite yet it's not...

The boy died and his mother went to Elisha for help. Elisha sent his servant to heal the boy, but he couldn't do it. End of story.

Elisha hadn't given up just yet...

Read 2 Kings 4 v 32-37

and use these backwards words to show what happened.

ydob	dewob	yob
hcuoc	daed	rood	seye
doG	dnuorg	yal	deyarp
moor	dezeens	dehcterts
deklaw	mraw

Elisha found the boy
d_____ on his c_____.
He shut the d_____ and
p_____ to G_____.
Then he l_____ on top
of the b_____. The boy's
b_____ grew w_____.
Elisha w_____
around the r_____, then
s_____ himself out
on the boy again. The boy
s_____ seven times
and opened his e_____!
The boy's mother was
amazed and b_____
down to the g_____.

That's incredible! But it wasn't down to Elisha. It was **God** who brought the boy back to life. Only God has power over life and death.

Jesus can give people life after death. If we trust Him to, Jesus can forgive our sins and give us eternal life with God.

Pray!

Thank God that He offers us eternal life. Pray for people you know who haven't yet accepted this amazing gift from God.

Stew-icide

**2 Kings
4 v 38-41**

*If you were
making a stew,
which of these
ingredients
would you put
in it?*

beef ☐

potatoes ☐

turnips ☐

broccoli ☐

rolling veg ☐

carrots ☐

salt ☐

pepper ☐

poison ☐

WEIRD WORDS

**Wild gourd
plant**
Some kind of
wild vegetable plant

Read 2 Kings 4 v 38

These guys must have been really
looking forward to some tasty stew.
Especially as there was a famine in
the area.

Unfortunately, one of the cooks
wasn't too fussy about what went
into the pot. He was probably
happy to use anything he could find
because of the food shortage.

Read verses 39-40

*and tick the kind of comments that
must have been flying around the
dinner table.*

Mmmm...
nice stew!

Are you
trying to kill
us?

I can't eat
that!

Can I have
the recipe?

Ugh! That
tastes of old
socks!

There was only one thing they could
do with the stew… ditch it!

But hold on! Elisha, the miracle-
working man of God, had other
plans…

Read verse 41

What did he put in the stew?

☐

It's pretty ordinary stuff. You can't
do much with it except make pastry,
or flour bombs. But in God's hands,
ordinary flour can make poisonous
stew edible!

We don't often like to bother
God with our ordinary everyday
problems. We think He isn't really
interested in us, and has more
important stuff to do. So when
things go wrong, we just moan
about it or get upset.

Action!

Next time, how about talking
to God? He cares. He can do
something about it.
And He often uses something
ordinary to sort things out for us.
Try talking to God now.

Feeding time

**2 Kings
4 v 42-44**

Through lots of miracles, God was showing the people that Elisha was His messenger.

So they should listen to him.

Here's another mind-blowing miracle...

Read 2 Kings 4 v 42-44

Go back one letter (B=A, C=B etc) to complete the story.

Elisha was in the town of

_ _ _ _ _ _, where
  H j m h b m

there was a _ _ _ _ _ _ _.
           g b n j o f

There was food in _ _ _ _
                C b b m

_ _ _ _ _ _ _ _ _.
  T i b m j t i b i

A man came from there bringing Elisha 20

_ _ _ _ _ _ of barley
m p b w f t   bread.

_ _ _ _ _ _ told him to
F m j t i b

give it to the _ _ _ _ _ _.
               q f p q m f

Even though there were 100

_ _ _, everyone _ _ _ _
n f o   b u f

enough and there was some

_ _ _ _ _ _ _ _!
m f g u   p w f s

The man knew there was a famine in Gilgal, so he took some food to Elisha.

Action!

Write down some of the ways you can help people who are having a tough time.

- •
- •
- •
- •
- •

God often uses the little things we do to achieve loads more than we expected! (Check out **Mark 8 v 1-9** for a similar story—we read about it on Day 11.)

Wow!

The miracles we've been reading about show God's great power, and His love for His people. But the Israelites needed to listen to God and turn back to living His way.

Pray!

Thank God for some of the things He's given you. And ask Him to help you live for Him.

2 Kings
5 v 1-12

Naaman

Skin deep

Read 2 Kings 5 v 1-3

Which of these describes Naaman?
a) **Army commander** ☐
b) **Highly respected** ☐
c) **Brave soldier** ☐

They all describe him! So what was the problem?
a) **He had no friends** ☐
b) **He had bad breath** ☐
c) **He had leprosy** ☐

This guy had everything. But if he wasn't cured of leprosy, he would suffer and probably die.

What did the slave girl do?
a) **Told him about Elisha** ☐
b) **Kept quiet** ☐
c) **Tickled him** ☐

This girl had been captured by Naaman's people. Yet she told Naaman (her enemy) about God's prophet. Amazing!

Wow!

Lots of people we know need a cure too! If their sin isn't sorted out, when they die they'll be separated from God for ever. But we can tell them that Jesus has the cure.

Read verse 4-8

The king of Israel thought that the king of Aram was picking a fight with him! He should have known that God's prophet **Elisha** could help Naaman. But the king had no trust in God.

Read verses 9-12

Elisha told Naaman to wash himself _____ times in the _____ and he would be cured.

Naaman couldn't believe it. Wash in the smelly Jordan? Surely God would cure him in a magical, spectacular way. He was furious.

Wow!

We often want God to answer our prayers in a big, spectacular way. But He can often use small things to make a **BIG** difference in our lives.

Pray!

Read the **Wow!** sections again. Anything you need to talk to God about? Go on then....

WEIRD WORDS

Aram
Country near Israel

Valiant
Brave

Leprosy
Nasty disease where your skin goes all lumpy and falls off

Ten talents
340kg of silver!

6000 shekels
69kg of gold!

Jordan
Main river in Israel

Cleansed
Cured, made clean

Damascus
Capital city of Aram

Wash and go!

**2 Kings
5 v 13-19**

*Will Naaman
listen to Elisha
and wash in the
River Jordan to
cure his leprosy?*

WEIRD WORDS

Cleansed
Clean and free from
disease

Attendants
Servants

Mules
Animals that are half
horse, half donkey

**Burnt offerings
and sacrifices**
Cooked meat offered
as a gift to God

Rimmon
False god, also
known as Baal

Read 2 Kings 5 v 13-15

Then fill in the vowels (aeiou).

Naaman's s____rv____nts
persuaded him to w___sh in
the R___v___r J___rd___n
When he did, his sk___n
was completely cured!

Naaman said: "Now I kn___w
that the G___d of
___sr___ ___l is the ___nly
G___d in the wh___l___
w___rld!"

Naaman knew that God had cured
him. He realised that God is in
control of everything!

Read verses 15 and 16

N___ ___m___n wanted to
p___y Elisha for curing him.
But Elisha r___f___s___d to
___cc___pt anything.

Wow!

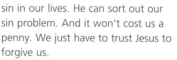

God can cure us too. We
need to get rid of the
sin in our lives. He can sort out our
sin problem. And it won't cost us a
penny. We just have to trust Jesus to
forgive us.

Read verses 17-19

Naaman wanted to take
loads of ___ ___rth back
home with him. It was a
sign that he now
w___rsh___pp___d the L___rd
alone and not other g___ds.

Naaman's boss was
the King of Aram, who
worshipped R__mm__n.
Naaman felt bad about
going to the t__mpl__ with
him. But __l__sh__ sent him
on his way in p__ __c__.

When God cures our sin problem,
our lives are **changed** like
Naaman's. We live only for God and
nothing else. Like Naaman, we'll still
get things wrong. But that's okay if
we keep learning to live for God!

Pray!

Ask God to change your life so
that you live more for Him.

Gehazi's grubby greed

God cured Naaman's leprosy, so Naaman wanted to give Elisha a present to say thanks.

But Elisha wouldn't accept it because God's cure was free.

WEIRD WORDS

Aramean
From Aram

Talent of silver
About 34kg

Pierced
Hurt

Griefs
Sadness

However, someone did want to get his grubby hands on Naaman's money...

Read 2 Kings 5 v 20-27
The blocks below tell Gehazi's story. Cross out the two blocks that are not in the story.

> **Gehazi thought "I can get something out of Naaman" (v20).**

> **But he changed his mind and went home for his dinner (v21).**

> **He ran after Naaman and told him a whopping big lie (v22).**

> **Naaman gave Gehazi 3 pigs, 5 turnips, 27 shuttlecocks and a jar of marmite (v24).**

> **Naaman gave Gehazi the money and clothes he asked for (v23).**

> **When he got home, Gehazi told Elisha another big lie! (v25)**

> **Because of his greed, Gehazi and his family all got leprosy (v27).**

*Check out what **1 Timothy 6 v 10** says about money.*

The love of _____

_____

_____ **evil.**

Now tick the boxes that are true.

Gehazi
Worked for God's prophet ☐

Knew about God ☐

Saw loads of miracles ☐

You
Know about God ☐

Read the Bible ☐

Go to church ☐

All 3 things about Gehazi were true, but he still disobeyed God. He put himself first, not God.

How many boxes did you tick? Feeling pretty holy?

Think!

Do all these things (reading your Bible, etc.) make any difference to how you live?
Do you live for God and obey Him? Or do you live just for yourself, as Gehazi did?
Ask God to help you live for Him.

44

2 Kings 6 v 1-7

Q: Which of these objects won't float?

Football

Sponge

Rubber duck

Iron axe

A:_____

Happy with your answer? Then get ready to think again...

WEIRD WORDS

Company of the prophets
Group of men who served God

Man of God
Elisha

Axe of faith

Elisha was the leader of a group of prophets. But their meeting hall was starting to get a little overcrowded...

Read 2 Kings 6 v 1-4

So far so good. They all went down to the River Jordan and started collecting wood for a new place for the prophets.

Read verses 5-7

What happened to the axe-head?
a) It melted in the sun ☐
b) It fell into the water ☐
c) A crocodile ate it ☐

Why was the guy so upset?
a) He'd borrowed it ☐
b) It was his fave axe ☐
c) He forgot to feed the cat ☐

In those days an iron axe-head was expensive. The man who lost it would have to go and work for the owner just to pay him back!

What did Elisha do?
a) **Told the man off** ☐
b) **Pushed him in the river** ☐
c) **Made the axe-head float** ☐

God cared enough about this man's sadness to do an amazing miracle through Elisha and get the axe-head back!

Wow!

God cares for His people (Christians). He sees when we're sad and when we're struggling with life. He's interested in even the small things in our lives!

Think!

Is something on your mind at the moment? What is it?

_____

_____

_____

_____

Pray!

Don't think it's too small for God to be bothered with. He wants to be involved in your life! Turn to Him for help right now.

**2 Kings
6 v 8-17**

*History File:
The Israelites
were God's
special people.*

*He'd promised
to be faithful
to them and
protect them.*

*Their part of
the deal was to
obey His laws.*

WEIRD WORDS

Conferring
Discussing

Enraged
Made him furious

Angry Aram v Angel army

Israel's enemy, the king of Aram, was making battle plans.

Read 2 Kings 6 v 8-9

and complete the king's plan.

Aram's Battle Plan

1. Make w_____ with Israel

2. Set up c_____ in such and such a place

3. Ambush the Is_____s

Sounds like a good plan...

Read verses 9-12

God scuppered the king's plans to defeat God's people! He told Elisha where the Arameans were hiding, and Elisha warned the Israelites.

Brilliant!

Read verses 13-17

Where was Elisha?

D_____

The king of Aram sent his huge army to surround Elisha and capture him. *What did Elisha's servant say (v15)?*

He was scared stiff! *But what did Elisha say (v16)?*

Elisha knew that God was on their side. And God showed Elisha's servant that His heavenly army was protecting them!

Wow!
Read Romans 8 v 31

Christians know that even when everyone seems to be against them, the power of God is on their side! God is always with them!

Pray!

Thank God that He is always with us. With Him on our side, we have nothing to fear. God is more powerful than anything!

Fight or feast?

**2 Kings
6 v 18-23**

What's going on?

Well, the king of Aram's massive army has surrounded Elisha to capture him.

But Elisha knows that he can't lose because God is on his side.

WEIRD WORDS

Samaria
City in Israel where the king lived

Bands from Aram
Groups of men from Aram who would raid Israel, capturing slaves

But first, another story.

Lauren was beaten up at school because she's a Christian. Her (very big) brother is furious and wants to teach the bullies a lesson. But Lauren says, "We should just forgive them. God doesn't want us to take revenge on people.".

What's your opinion of this situation?

a) Lauren's brother is right ☐
b) Lauren must be stupid ☐
c) She did the right thing ☐

Okay, now let's find out what Elisha did when the army came to capture him. Remember, the king of Aram would probably have killed Elisha.

Read 2 Kings 6 v 18-21

What do you think Elisha will say?

a) Kill them all! ☐
b) Just torture them a bit ☐
c) Let them off and give them a fantastic feast ☐

Read verses 22-23

Elisha told the king to feed them! And the army from Aram stopped attacking Israel. Great result!

Complete these great lines from Romans 12 v 20-21.

**If your enemy is hungry,
_____. If he is
thirsty, _____
_____.**

**Don't be overcome by
evil, but defeat evil with
_____.**

Wow!

The army from Aram saw that God was in control. If we follow Elisha's and Lauren's examples, people will start to notice that God is in control of our lives.

Pray!

Ask God to help you show kindness to people, even to those who are nasty towards you or bug you.

Believe it or not

God keeps protecting the Israelites. But their king, Joram, refuses to turn to God or trust His prophet, Elisha.

WEIRD WORDS

Mobilised
Got them ready for battle

Laid siege
Surrounded

80 shekels
Nearly 1kg of silver!

Cab
About 100g

Seed pods
Probably bird dung

Seah
About 7 litres

Shekel
12g of silver

Read 2 Kings 6 v 24-31

The siege had a terrible effect on Samaria. No food was coming into the city and the people were starving.

> **What were people selling for lots of money (v25)?**
>
> **What worse things were happening (v28)?**
>
> **How did the king react (v30)?**
>
> **Who did he blame (v31)?**

Read 2 Kings 6 v 32 – 7 v 2

> **Who was King Joram really blaming (v33)?**
>
> **How soon did Elisha say things would get better (v1)?**
>
> **Did they believe God could do this (v2)?**

Hideous stuff. Ben-Hadad trapped the people in Samaria for so long that they ran out of food. Donkey's heads and "seed pods" were being sold as food for huge amounts of money. People were killing and eating their children. Disgusting.

The Israelites were desperate; yet the king still didn't turn to God for help. But God would rescue them anyway. Elisha said God would improve the situation the very next day! But the king's servant refused to believe it, so God would punish him for his lack of faith.

Wow!

Faith in God means believing what He's promised. God promises to rescue everyone who believes Jesus died in their place. Those who refuse to believe it will be punished. Those of us who do believe will be rescued by God and will live for ever with Him!

Pray!

Ask God to help you believe His promises in the Bible.

Famine and fortune

**2 Kings
7 v 3-20**

Samaria, the capital of Israel, was under siege from the Arameans.

The Israelites were starving and close to death.

But God promised that things would change very quickly...

WEIRD WORDS

Plight
Bad situation

Plundered
Took possessions from a defeated enemy

Read 2 Kings 7 v 3-20

Use the wordsearch to find words missing from the story.

P	L	U	N	D	E	R	E	D	Z	R A
S	R	Q	L	U	V	T	B	C	E	J U
F	L	O	U	R	R	N	S	V	Q	A T
E	R	S	M	J	D	V	L	U	P	R R
L	V	E	V	I	C	I	T	Y	U	A A
I	B	H	O	R	S	E	S	C	A	M P
S	A	T	U	N	Q	E	W	E	T	E V
H	R	O	X	W	G	O	D	U	O	A P
A	L	L	C	B	M	X	R	R	L	N N
M	E	C	H	A	R	I	O	T	S	S Z
F	Y	S	O	R	P	E	L	Y	M	Q Y
G	N	I	K	J	T	E	U	N	E	W S

God used four men with
l_____ to discover
that the A_____
had run away. This enemy
army heard the sound of
c_____ and
h_____ and panicked.
The L_____ had scared
them away! The lepers
took s_____, gold
and c_____ from
the enemy camp. Then they
went back to the c_____
and reported the good
n_____. The k_____
thought it was
a clever t_____ by the
Arameans. But soldiers
discovered the report was
t_____. The people left the
city and p_____
the enemy c_____.

The price of f_____
and b_____went
down, just as G_____
had promised. The king's
servant who refused to
believe E_____ was
killed, just as God had
p_____.

As often happens in the Bible, God used outsiders in His great plans. God had terrified the Arameans (v6-7), and then these lowly lepers delivered the good news. Time and time again, God uses the weak in His plans.

God kept His promise to rescue the people, and also to punish the unbelieving officer (v19-20). God always keeps His word — to rescue His people and punish those who refuse to believe.

Think!

Ever think God couldn't use you? Ever look down on other people as useless? Ever doubt God's word?

Pray!

Talk these things over with God, asking Him to change your attitude.

God's great timing

46

**2 Kings
8 v 1-6**

Remember the woman from Shunem? She kindly built a room in her house for Elisha.

God gave her a baby boy and yet the boy died. But God used Elisha to bring him back to life.

Remember her? Well, she's back!

WEIRD WORDS

Decreed
Ordered

Assigned
Appointed

Read 2 Kings 8 v 1-2

Fill in the missing letters to show the great advice Elisha gave.

Go away with your f_m__ly because the L__rd has ordered f__m__n__ in the area. It will last for s__v__n y__ __rs.

She took his advice and they moved away for seven years. But while she was away someone took her house and land.

Read verses 3-6

Now complete the conversation between the king and Gehazi.

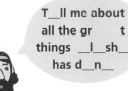

T__ll me about all the gr__ __t things __l__sh__ has d__n__

Look! Here's the w__m__n whose s__n Elisha r_st__r__d back to l_f__!

Your Majesty, please give me back my h__ __se and l__nd!

Make sure __v__ryth__ng that belonged to her is g__v__n back to her. Including any m__n__y owed her from her l__nd while she was out of the c__ __ntry.

Great timing from God. Just as Gehazi was telling the king about her, the woman showed up to beg for her land back. The king could see for himself the boy that God (through Elisha) had brought back to life.

After hearing all about God's grace, the king responded in the right way by showing grace and generosity to the woman and her family.

Action!

How have you seen God's generosity in your life?

_____

_____

So how can you show such kindness to someone else?

_____

_____

Ask God to help you do it!

Mark: Who is Jesus?

**Mark
8 v 22-26**

*Back to Mark's
book about Jesus.*

*The disciples
haven't yet
realised who Jesus
is — God's Son.*

*And they're not
the only blind
people Jesus
meets...*

*Use the word
pool to complete
the story.*

Read Mark 8 v 22-25

spat   people   deaf
cloudily   touched   Jesus
Bethsaida   touch   see
clearly   pillows   blind
turnips   trees   eyes
village   vegetable

**Jesus and His disciples
reached B_____.
Some people brought along
a b_____ man and
asked J_____ to
t_____ him. Jesus
took the man outside of the
v_____, s_____
on the man's e_____
and touched him. *"Do you
s_____ anything?"* asked
Jesus. *"I see p_____
but they look like walking
t_____."* Then Jesus
t_____ the man's
eyes again. He was healed
and could see everything
c_____.**

Jesus has the power to heal people.
Miracles like this point us to the fact
that Jesus is God's Son, the Messiah/
Christ. But this miracle was also a
picture of the disciples (and of us
too!).

The disciples did not see who Jesus
really was. They needed God to
help them see clearly. In tomorrow's
Bible bit, Peter starts to see the truth
about Jesus...

Think!

Lots of people can't see
who Jesus really is — the Messiah/
Christ, who can rescue them
from their sinful ways. Have YOU
understood who Jesus is?

Read verse 26

Jesus didn't want everyone to
know what He'd done. It wasn't
time for His enemies to catch up
with Him yet...

Pray!

Think of people you know who
don't understand who Jesus really
is. Ask God to open their eyes
so they realise they need Jesus in
their lives.

WEIRD WORDS

Bethsaida
Town near the Sea
of Galilee

**Mark
8 v 27-30**

Mark has given us loads of evidence that Jesus is the Messiah/Christ.

***Messiah** and **Christ** are the same name. They both mean the King who God promised would come to rescue His people.*

Uncovering evidence

Unscramble the anagrams to uncover the evidence.

M_____
RIMACLES
(Mark 6 v 41)

Jesus did many amazing things. He healed loads of people, drove out evil spirits and even fed thousands of people from a tiny amount of food. These were all signs pointing to the fact that Jesus was the Christ.

T_____
CHEATING
(Mark 4 v 1)

Jesus told great parables — stories that explained big truths. Yet the people who heard His teaching still didn't realise who He was!

Read Mark 8 v 27-28
Who did people think Jesus was?

J_____   T_____
HONJ   HET

B_____
BATSPIT

Wrong! John actually came before Jesus. He prepared the way for Jesus by showing people that they needed to turn away from sin.

E_____
HEJAIL
Wrong again!

Finally, someone worked it out...

Read verses 29-30

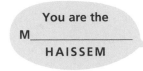
You are the
M_____
HAISSEM

Peter realised that Jesus was the King who had come to rescue God's people.

Who do you think Jesus is?

Just a good man ☐
A fake ☐
The Messiah – my Rescuer ☐
I don't really care ☐

Now talk to God about your answer.

For the free e-booklet
What's it all about?, email
discover@thegoodbook.co.uk
or check out
www.thegoodbook.co.uk/contact-us
to find our UK mailing address.

Born to die

**Mark
8 v 31-33**

Finally, Peter worked out that Jesus was the Messiah/Christ — the Rescuer sent by God!

But what had Jesus Christ actually come to do?

Read Mark 8 v 31

Many people expected the Messiah to be a warrior who would bash the Romans. *But what did Jesus say would happen to Him? Fill in the vowels to reveal the truth.*

• The S___n of M___n must s___ff___r m___ny th___ngs

• He'll be r___j___ct___d by the ___ld___rs, ch___ ___f pr___ ___sts and t___ ___ch___rs of the l___w

• He must be k___ll___d

• But He will r___s___ again after thr___ ___ days

Read verse 32

Peter couldn't understand why Jesus was talking about suffering and dying. Surely that wouldn't happen to God's Son?!! So Peter told Jesus off for talking like that. Bad move!

Read verse 33

What did Jesus say to Peter?

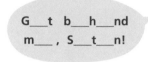

G___t b___h___nd m___ , S___t___n!

Peter wanted to persuade Jesus not to die. But it was all part of **God's plan** that Jesus would die. God sent His Son, Jesus, into the world to rescue people from sin. And that would mean dying to take the punishment for that sin.

Satan (the devil) wants to spoil God's plans, and he was trying to do that through Peter here. That's why Jesus called Peter *Satan* for not wanting Him to die. Jesus came to earth to die on the cross, and not even the devil would stop Him.

WEIRD WORDS

Son of Man
Jesus

Elders, chief priests and teachers of the law
The people most expected to welcome the Messiah

Rebuke
Tell off

Wow!

That's not what people expected from the Messiah. But Jesus knew that dying on the cross and being raised back to life was the only way to rescue people from sin.

Pray!

Jesus came into the world to die.
In our place. For our sins.
Spend time thanking and praising Him right now.

Carry your cross

In the box up there, quickly scribble what you think being a Christian involves.

Let's see if Jesus agrees…

Read Mark 8 v 34-37
What does Jesus say His followers (Christians) must do? Go back one letter to find out.

E F O Z

Z P V S T F M G

That means stop putting yourself first. Christians have Jesus in charge of their lives. So they live to please Him, not themselves.

Action!

How can you put Jesus first? (Give up something to spend more time with Jesus? Try talking to Him every day?)

_____

_____

_____

Read verse 34 again

WEIRD WORDS

The gospel
The great news that Jesus can rescue us

Forfeit
Give up, lose

Soul
Whole life. In verses 36-37 Jesus is saying: *"What's the point of living for yourself, refusing to accept me, and so not gaining eternal life?"*

U B L F   V Q

Z P V S   D S P T T

Jesus carried His cross on His way to die in our place. And He expects His followers to be prepared to die for Him!

Wow!

In your country, people are probably not often killed for following Jesus! But when Christians tell people about Jesus, they can expect to suffer teasing, losing friends, or hassle from family. Being a Christian can be really hard work! But Jesus went through far worse to rescue us!

Pray!

Ask God to give you the strength to follow Jesus, put up with the hard times, and tell people about Jesus. Ask Him to help you do the stuff you wrote in the *Action!* section.

51

**Mark
8 v 38 – 9 v 1**

*Jesus has told His
followers that
they must put
Him first in their
lives.*

*And be prepared
to suffer for
following Him.*

*And that's not
all...*

Shame game

*Ever get embarrassed about being a
Christian? Find it hard to stick up for
Jesus when people say bad things
about Him? Keep quiet about going
to church?*

Check out Jesus' strong words.

Read Mark 8 v 38 – 9 v 1

Wow!

People who are ashamed of
Jesus, and choose to live for
themselves instead of Him,
will not be rescued from sin
by Him. When Jesus returns to earth
on the Day of Judgement, He'll have
nothing to do with people who've
rejected Him.

Now read Romans 1 v 16

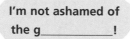

> **I'm not ashamed of
> the g_____!**

The gospel is the good news about
Jesus. *Read back from the end to
find out why Paul's not ashamed.*

**SEVEILEBOHWENOYREVE
OTNOITAVLAS
SGNIRBTAHT
DOGFOREWOPEHTSITI**

It_____

_____

_____

_____

If you're a Christian, Jesus died for
you! You've had all your wrongs
forgiven by Him. In fact, anyone
who turns to Him can be rescued
from sin! Why would we be
ashamed of that??? Surely we want
to tell as many people as possible!

But it can be really hard admitting
you're a Christian or telling friends
about Jesus. But the more you do it,
the easier it gets. When people ask
you what you did at the weekend,
mention church. When they ask you
if you're a Christian, say "Yes!" and
tell them why.

> **What did you
> do yesterday?**

> **I played tennis,
> then went to
> youth group.
> Great fun!**

Pray!

Ask God to help you not to be
ashamed of Him, giving you
courage to talk about Jesus.

*For a fact sheet on telling friends about
Jesus, email or write to the address found
on Day 48.*

*For a fact sheet on telling friends about
Jesus, email or write to the address found
on Day 48.*

WEIRD WORDS

**Adulterous and
sinful generation**
People who rejected
God

Son of Man
Jesus

Salvation
Rescue from sin

**Mark
9 v 2-8**

*Ever stood
on top of a
mountain?*

*The view is
spectacular.*

*Peter, James
and John saw
something even
more amazing
at the top of
this mountain…*

WEIRD WORDS

Elijah
Old Testament
prophet who came
before Elisha

Rabbi
Teacher

Transfigure it out

Read Mark 9 v 2-4

What did they see?

**1. J___s___s was
tr__nsf__g__r__d**

That means His appearance
changed, to reveal His glory.

**2. His cl___th___s became
d__zzl__ng wh__t__**

**3. El__j__h and M__s__s
talked to Jesus**

Two great men who served God in
Old Testament times. But Jesus is far
greater than even these two! Jesus
is God's Son.

Read verses 5-6

Peter was so scared that he blurted
out the first thing that came into
his head! But someone else had
something to say…

Read verses 7-8

The voice in the cloud was God
Himself! *What did He say?*

> **This is my S___n,
> whom I l___ve**

So Jesus really is God's Son.

What else did God say?

> **L___st___n to
> H___m!**

And He wants us to do the same!

Wow!

That means: reading
more about Jesus in the
Bible; staying awake
and listening in church and youth
meetings; acting on what we learn.

Action!

Here's a way to
help you listen and
learn from what Jesus says. Grab
a notebook and rename it your
"Jesus File". Split each page up like
the example below. Every time you
read about Jesus in the Bible or
hear about Him in a meeting, fill in
a page.

Bible passage:
What it says about Jesus or what Jesus teaches:
What I've learned:
What I'm going to do about it:

Pray!

Ask God to help you to listen to
Jesus and to learn from what He
says.

Elijah the second?

Mark
9 v 9-13

Peter, James and John have just seen an amazing thing happen to Jesus.

And God Himself told them to listen to Jesus!

Here's their first chance to do just that…

Read Mark 9 v 9-10

Circle the 2 things Jesus told them.

Tell everyone about this

Don't tell anyone what you have seen yet

Why did the chicken cross the road?

The Son of Man will rise from death

I'm fed up with you following me all the time!

He told them to keep quiet because they still didn't fully understand who Jesus was and why He had come. They would only understand once He had died and had been raised back to life.

Who else had the disciples seen with Jesus on the mountain (v4)?

_____ and _____

Seeing Elijah up on the mountain with Jesus reminded them of something that didn't seem to make sense. **Read verse 11.**

The Old Testament says that Elijah would come again before the Christ. Do a quick flick to **Malachi 4 v 5** on the last page of the Old Testament. But what does that mean?

Read verses 12-13

Jesus said that this Elijah had come already! But not the same Elijah we read about yesterday. Someone who taught in the same fiery way as Elijah. *Cross out the **ELIJAHs** to reveal all.*

J O H E L I J A H N T H E B

E L I J A H A P T E L I J A H I S T

J_____

_____ **(Matthew 17v12–13)**

John the Baptist came before Jesus, telling people to turn away from their sins. He had prepared the way for Jesus to come and die for people's sins.

WEIRD WORDS

Son of Man
Jesus — as well as being God's Son, He was a human being

Pray!

Jesus wanted His disciples to understand who He was and why He had come to earth. Ask God to help you to understand these things about Jesus.

Pray it cool

*Peter, James
and John are
on their way
back down the
mountain with
Jesus.*

*But what's all
that noise?*

WEIRD WORDS

**Possessed by
a spirit**
An evil spirit
(demon) was
making the boy ill

*Use the wordsearch to find today's
missing words.*

```
D B J A R G U I N G
R I X H J E S U S R
I K S P I R I T G O
V Q U C O V F E M U
E R E B I G P A O N
G G F N F P A C U D
C R O W D R L H T M
O E A D S A H E H D
O E M Y E Y C R S L
Z T L O D Z T S O N
```

Read Mark 9 v 14-15

The d_____
were surrounded by a large
c_____.
The t_____ of the
law were a_____
with them. When the people
saw J_____, they ran
to g_____ Him.

Read verses 16-18

The man's s_____ was
controlled by a s_____
which threw him to the
g_____ and made
him f_____ at the
m_____. The disciples
couldn't d_____ out
the spirit.

Read verses 28-29

**The disciples couldn't drive
out the spirit because they
didn't p_____.**

They had driven out evil spirits
before, so they probably assumed
they could do it any time. But they
could only do it with God's help,
and they hadn't prayed to Him
for help!

Want to tell your
friends about
Jesus?

Got exams
coming up?

Want to serve
God more?

Then you need to talk to
God in prayer, and rely on
Him to help you!

Pray!

What do you need God to help
you with? Talk to Him about it.

*Tomorrow: Can Jesus drive out the
evil spirit?*

Mission impossible?

**Mark
9 v 19-27**

*A boy has an
evil spirit in him
which is making
him really ill.*

*But the disciples
can't drive it out
of him...*

WEIRD WORDS

Convulsion
Shaking wildly

Rebuked
Told off

Mute
Unable to speak

Time for Jesus to show who's really
in control.

Read Mark 9 v 19-23

What did Jesus call the people?

Un_____

It upset Jesus that the people didn't
believe that He was God's Son, who
could do anything.

The boy's father

said, "**If** you can do anything, help
us". He wasn't sure if Jesus could
heal his son.

The disciples

hadn't turned to God in prayer or
trusted Him to help them heal the
boy.

The people

didn't realise who Jesus was. They
didn't believe that He'd come to
rescue them from sin. And some
didn't believe He could heal this boy.

*Now write out Jesus' words from
verse 23 (in the space at the top of
the page).*

Everything _____
_____
_____
_____
_____

Wow!

Anything is possible for us
when we believe, because
anything is possible for the one we
believe in — Jesus!

Read verses 24-27

The spirit obeyed Jesus and left the
boy! The boy's father **did** believe
that Jesus could heal his son, even
though he had been doubtful. He
showed he believed by asking Jesus
for help (v24).

Think!

It's not about how much
faith we have (phew!) but who we
put our faith in. Do you believe
Jesus can do amazing things in your
life?

Pray!

Thank God that anything is
possible if we believe in Him!

Genesis: God's promises

**Genesis
18 v 1-15**

Today we get back to Genesis and the story of Abraham.

God made three fantastic promises to Abraham. Flick back to Day 15 and read God's great promises.

Now the story continues...

Imagine you're watching TV and the doorbell rings. You open the door... and can't believe your eyes! At the door is _____
(fill in a surprise visitor).

Abraham had some surprise visitors. One of them was God!

Read Genesis 18 v 1-8

Abraham soon realised that one of his guests was God. The other two were angels. *What did Abraham do for his guests?*

- **B____ ____ down to the ground (v2)**
- **Gave them w_____ (v4)**
- **Let them r_____ under a t_____ (v4)**
- **Gave them lots to e_____ (v5)**

Think!

Do you look after people like that? Do you go out of your way to show friendship?

What about God? How do you treat Him? Do you give Him the respect He deserves?

Read verses 9-15

What promise did God make to Abraham (v10)?

> **I will come back next year and S_____ your wife will have a s_____.**

Sarah was listening in and didn't believe a word of it. Surely she was far too old to have a baby!

But nothing is too hard for God (v14). If He promised it, then Sarah *would* have a baby (wait until Day 62!). God can do anything!

Sarah made the mistake of lying to God (v15) to cover up her unbelief. But God knew the truth.

Pray!

We can't hide stuff from God! He knows everything we say, think or do.
Bearing that in mind, is there anything you want to say to God right now?

51

God's friend

**Genesis
18 v 16-33**

*Abraham is
entertaining
three surprise
visitors. One of
them is God!*

Time for a stroll...

WEIRD WORDS

Household
Family and servants

Grievous
Upsetting to God

The righteous
People who lived
God's way

Dust and ashes
Abraham knew that,
compared to God, he
was as unimportant
as dust!

Read Genesis 18 v 16-19

God and Abraham had a special
relationship. Abraham's descendants
would be God's chosen people
(the Israelites). God knew Abraham
would bring up his children to
follow God's ways.

**Isaiah 41 v 8 tells us that
God counted Abraham as His**

f _ _ _ _ _ !

That's why God told Abraham His
plans for two evil cities: Sodom and
Gomorrah…

Read verses 20-21

God was going to punish Sodom
and Gomorrah because they had
rejected Him and sinned against Him
in a big way. Abraham was so close
to God that the Lord even told him
His plans!

Wow!

It seems amazing to have
a friendship with the God
who made the whole universe!

But thanks to Jesus, we can be
friends with God too!

These cities deserved to be
destroyed. Just one problem —
Abraham's nephew Lot was living in
Sodom!

Sodom

Speed read verses 22-33

Abraham pleaded with God to save
Sodom, so that the godly people
living there (like Lot) wouldn't be
destroyed too.

*How many godly people did
there have to be for God to
spare the whole city (v32)?*

You can sense how desperate
Abraham was becoming as the
numbers he asked for got smaller
and smaller.

Wow!

God agreed! He is totally
fair. He punishes those
who reject Him, and yet rescues
everyone who turns to Him.

Pray!

Know anyone who needs God
to save them? People who aren't
friends with God? Plead with God
to rescue them.

58

**Genesis
19 v 1-11**

Lot

*God was going
to destroy the
evil city of
Sodom.*

*But Abraham
pleaded with
God to save his
nephew Lot.*

*So God sent two
angels to check
out the sinful
city.*

Lot in a hot spot

Read Genesis 19 v 1-3

Lot was kind to the angels, just as
Abraham had been. But they were
not safe for long.

Read verses 4-5

Horrible. The people of Sodom really
were sinful and godless. No wonder
God was so upset by their actions.

Read verses 6-8

*Fill in the vowels (aeiou) to show
what Lot did.*

**1. He t__ld the m___n not
to do such a w__ck__d
th__ng (v7)**

When people around us are doing
stuff we know is wrong, it's good
to try and talk them out of it. Even
when we know they'll probably
ignore us, it's good to make a stand.

**2. He offered the men his
tw__ d__ __ghters (v8)**

Unbelievable. How could he give up
his own daughters to these sinful
men? Lot had made a bad choice by
moving into sinful Sodom. Look at
the mess he was in now.

Read verses 9-11

God rescued Lot and his family from
this terrifying situation!

Wow!

Having the wrong circle
of friends can affect us
more than we think. Lot
was influenced by the sinful people
around him and he found himself in
a bad situation.

Think!

How are you affected by
the people around you?
Do you join in with the swearing,
offensive jokes, or bullying?

Pray!

Say sorry to God for specific times
when you've joined in with doing
the wrong thing. Ask Him to give
you the courage to stand up to
people around you when you
need to.

Word of warning

**Genesis
19 v 12-16**

*You wake up in
the middle of
the night, feeling
really warm.*

*You can also
smell smoke.*

*You hear a voice
shout, "The house
is on fire! Quick,
get out!"*

But you're sooo comfy in bed.
So you turn over and go back to
sleep. **How dumb would that
be?!! We can't ignore serious
warnings like that!**

Back to Lot in Sodom. God sent two
angels to destroy the sinful city. But
He also warned Lot to get out.

Read Genesis 19 v 12-14

*Use the code to reveal Lot's warning
to his relatives (v14).*

But the idiots ignored him!
Loads of people don't take God's
warnings in the Bible seriously.

*Decode this warning from Romans
6 v 23…*

Anyone who won't turn away from
sin and turn to God will be punished
by Him. But that's not the end of
the story…

Read verses 15-16

God offered Lot the chance to
be rescued and He offers us that
chance too (Romans 6 v 23).

Pray!

Thank God that He warns
everyone and gives them the
chance to be rescued from the
punishment for sin.

Don't ignore His warning!

WEIRD WORDS

Merciful
Showing
forgiveness when
it's not deserved

A B C D E F G H I J L N O R S T U W Y

Disaster strikes

**Genesis
19 v 17-29**

God sent two angels to destroy the sinful cities of Sodom and Gomorrah.

But will Lot, his wife and his daughters get out of Sodom in time?

WEIRD WORDS

Plain
Flat area of land where Sodom and Gomorrah were

Zoar
means *small*

Sulphur
A chemical that burns and destroys

1. God's care for Lot
Read Genesis 19 v 17-22

Fill in the Os to show what the angel said to Lot (v17).

"Run t___ the m___untains!"

But Lot didn't think he could make it to the mountains. So he asked if he could go to Zoar instead. God not only let Lot do that, but He also spared the town of Zoar.

2. God's punishment

Read verses 23-25

The L___rd destr___yed S__d__m and G__m__rrah

God had said He would destroy these cities because they had rejected Him and had sinned so badly. God cannot stand sin, and He rightly punishes it.

3. A terrible mistake
Read verses 17 and 26

What had the angel said?

"D___n't l___ ___k back!"

Maybe Lot's wife couldn't bear to leave Sodom. Or maybe she doubted God. Whatever the reason, she disobeyed God and paid the price.

God doesn't take sin lightly! It hurts Him when we disobey Him. That's why He treats sin so seriously.

4. God kept His promises
Read verses 27-29

and fill in the Rs and Bs.

**God ___emem___e___ed
A___ ___aham (v29)**

God remembered His promise to Abraham and rescued Lot from Sodom. God always keeps His promises!

Pray!

Thank God that He...
a) cares for His people
b) deals fairly with sin
c) always keeps His promises

61

Abraham slips up

**Genesis
20 v 1-18**

*Abraham and
Sarah are on the
move again...*

*To a place called
Gerar, where King
Abimelek hung
out.*

Read Genesis 20 v 1-2

**What was Abraham's
mistake?**
a) He cried about Sarah ☐
b) He lied about Sarah ☐
c) He cried about sausages ☐

Abraham was worried that Abimelek
would kill him and take Sarah for
himself. That's why Abraham lied
about her. But he'd made this
mistake once before (Genesis 12 v
11-13).

Think!

Is there something
wrong that you keep
on doing?

_____

_____

Talk to God about it and ask Him to
help you to fight the temptation.

Read Genesis 20 v 3-7

God said He would punish Abimelek
for taking Abraham's wife as his
own. But Abimelek told God that
he hadn't known that Sarah was
married.

What did God call Abraham?
a) A liar ☐
b) A professor ☐
c) A prophet ☐

Wow!

Despite Abraham messing
up, he was still God's
prophet. God doesn't turn
His back on His people when they
let Him down. He sticks by them to
the end. *Check out John 5 v 24.*

Read verses 8-18

Abraham had deceived Abimelek
because he was scared of him and
hadn't trusted God to keep him
safe.

It's easy to rely on ourselves rather
than turn to God for help. Yet He's
in control and should always be the
first person we turn to.

Pray!

Praise God that He never turns
away from His people (Christians).
Thank Him that you can turn to
Him with anything that's on your
mind. Do that right now.

WEIRD WORDS

**Clear conscience
and clean hands**
Abimelek had
nothing to feel
guilty about

Prophet
God's servant and
messenger

1000 shekels
12 kg of silver —
that's a lot!

Vindicated
Proved to be in
the right

**Genesis
21 v 1-7**

*For a recap, flick
back to Day 56.*

*God had visited
Abraham
and Sarah,
promising them
a baby.*

*Sarah had
laughed at this
ridiculous idea...*

WEIRD WORDS

Gracious
God gave Sarah
far more than she
deserved

Isaac
means *he laughs*

Circumcised
Cut off part of the
skin around the
penis. A sign of
God's covenant
with Abraham

Abe's babe

Read Genesis 21 v 1
and fill in the gap.

The Lord _____

_____ Sarah as

He had said

Sarah hadn't believed God, yet He
still gave her a son. And she was
over 90 years old!

Action!

God is so gracious to us.
Even though we let Him
down, He gives us much more than
we deserve.

On scrap paper, write a list of what
God has done for you (e.g. given
you great friends, helped you at
school).

Read verses 2-7

God was keeping His promises, even
though Abraham and Sarah had to
wait for them. Sarah had laughed
at the crazy idea of God giving her
a baby in her old age (Genesis 18
v 10-12). Now she was laughing
with **joy** because God had kept this
amazing promise.

**Earlier in Genesis, God
had made a covenant
(agreement) with Abraham.
Abraham had promised to
live for God, and God had
promised him three things.**

To reveal them, go back 1 letter.

‾ ‾ ‾ ‾
M B O E

One day, God would give
Abraham's family (the Israelites) the
land of Canaan.

‾ ‾ ‾ ‾ ‾ ‾ ‾
D I J M E S F O

Abraham was 100, yet God kept His
promise of a son. And Abraham's
family would grow into the huge
Israelite nation. God's people!

‾ ‾ ‾ ‾ ‾ ‾
C M F T T J O H

Through Abraham's family, God
would bless the whole world. **Jesus**
would be a descendant of Abraham
and Isaac. Jesus would make it
possible for **anyone** to get right
with God.

Pray!

Thank God that He kept His
covenant promises. Spend time
praising Him for the things you
wrote down earlier.

Family fall out

**Genesis
21 v 8-21**

*God kept His
promise.*

*Abraham and
Sarah had a baby
(Isaac) when they
were about 100
years old!*

*Everyone was so
happy when Isaac
was born.*

*Well, nearly
everyone...*

WEIRD WORDS

Weaned
Moved on from milk
to solid food

**Offspring will be
reckoned**
Only Isaac's
descendants would
be part of God's
people

Read Genesis 21 v 8-13
and cross out the wrong words.

**Abraham had also had a
son with Hagar/Hagrid/
Haggis. He was called Isaiah/
Ishmael. Sarah hated Hagar
and Ishmael so she told
Abraham to kill them / kick
them out. Abraham didn't
want to, but God told him to
listen to Sally/Sarah/Susan.**

Isaac was the son God had promised
Abraham. It was through Isaac and
his descendants (the Israelites) that
God would bless the whole world.
Not Ishmael.

Read verses 14-16

**Abraham gave them food
and water. Then they went
out into the dentist's/desert.
But they ran out of water/
watermelons so Hagar
left Ishmael under a bush/
cushion to die.**

Hold on a minute! God had
promised to protect Ishmael and
give him loads of children. So what's
going on???

Read verses 17-21

**God heard Ishmael crying
and sent an aardvark/angel
to them. The angel reminded
Hagar of God's possum/
promise. God opened her
eyes so that she saw a
wheel/well/welshman and
gave Ishmael a drink/sink
to keep him alive. God was
with Ishmael as he grew up.**

God kept His promise to Hagar
and Ishmael! Even though Ishmael
wasn't the son God had promised
Abraham, God still cared for him.

Pray!

1. Thank God that He always
   keeps His promises.
2. Thank Him that He cares for
   people no matter who they are
   or where they're from.
3. Praise Him that He sent Jesus
   to the whole world and not
   just to the Israelites.

Abe gets it right

Genesis
21 v 22-34

God has promised to give Abraham the land he's living in. But he doesn't own it yet, so Abe's living in danger.

There are 2 ways he can respond:

1. Be cowardly and sinful
2. Be courageous and godly

It's hard being godly when so many people around us aren't.

4000 years ago, Abraham struggled with the same thing.

1. Be cowardly and sinful

Three days ago we read about Abraham messing up. He was scared of King Abimelek and pretended that Sarah wasn't his wife so Abimelek wouldn't kill him and steal his wife. It was the wrong thing to do. Abraham was cowardly and sinned rather than having the courage to live God's way.

Think!

Do you ever do the wrong thing rather than have the courage to live God's way and trust Him to help you out?

WEIRD WORDS

Abimelek
The king

Treaty
Peace agreement

Beersheba
Means *"well of the oath"*

Tamarisk tree
Small desert tree

Eternal
Everlasting

Read Genesis 21 v 22-34

Then number the events in the order they happened.

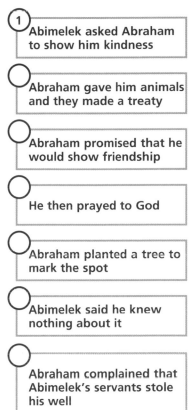

(1) **Abimelek asked Abraham to show him kindness**

○ **Abraham gave him animals and they made a treaty**

○ **Abraham promised that he would show friendship**

○ **He then prayed to God**

○ **Abraham planted a tree to mark the spot**

○ **Abimelek said he knew nothing about it**

○ **Abraham complained that Abimelek's servants stole his well**

2. Be courageous and godly

This time Abraham did the right thing. He was kind and generous to Abimelek. He didn't resort to lies, and he trusted God to look after him. And, of course, God did!

Pray!

Ask God for the courage to live in a way that pleases Him. So that you don't take the cowardly, sinful option, but treat people in a godly way.

65

**Genesis
22 v 1-10**

*What's the
hardest choice
you've had to
make this week?*

*Which music to
listen to?*

*What to get your
mum for her
birthday?*

*Which socks to
wear?*

The toughest test

Abraham was about to face the hardest choice of his long life.

Read Genesis 2 v 1-2

Unjumble the anagrams to reveal what God asked Abraham to do.

Take your son I_____,
a c a s l

whom you I_____, to the
o v e l

region of M_____.
r i o h a M

Sacrifice him there as a
b_____ offering on one
t r u n b

of the m_____
m a i n s n o u t

Abraham often made sacrifices to God. He would kill an animal or bird, cook it, and offer it to God. It was a way of saying sorry or thank you to God. But this time God told Abraham to sacrifice his own son!

What an impossibly hard decision to make. Abraham had waited so long to have a son, and now he was being asked to sacrifice him!

God was testing Abraham. Did he really trust God? Did he love God even more than his own son?

What would Abraham do?

Read verses 3-10

A_____ and Isaac
A h a m b a r

carried the w_____ up the
d o w o

mountain. Abraham built an

a_____, tied up I_____
t a r a l   c a s l a

and laid him on the altar. He

then took a k_____ to
i f k e n

kill his son.

Abraham was really going to kill his son! He showed that he loved and trusted God more than anything else. He still loved Isaac, but God came first.

Pray!

Ask God to help you to love Him as much as Abraham did. To trust Him completely. To obey Him.

WEIRD WORDS

**Sacrifice /
Burnt offering**
See box

Altar
Table where
sacrifices were
killed and burnt

So, did Abraham actually kill Isaac? Find out tomorrow...

On a knife edge...

**Genesis
22 v 9-19**

*God told
Abraham to
sacrifice his son
Isaac to show
how much
he loved and
trusted God.*

*Would Abraham
plunge the
knife into his
son or not?*

WEIRD WORDS

Thicket
Thorny hedge

Ram
Male sheep

Offspring
Descendants,
children

Read Genesis 22 v 9-12

God stopped Abraham from killing Isaac! God saw that Abraham really did love Him and trust Him above anything else. He wouldn't hold anything back from God, not even his own son.

Think!

What do you hold back from God? Your time? Your money? Your love? What are you going to do about it?

_____

_____

_____

The sacrifice still had to be made.

Read verses 13-14

God provided a sheep to take Isaac's place. Later on in the Bible, John the Baptist said that the Lamb of God would *"take away the sin of the world"* (John 1 v 29). The Lamb of God is Jesus.

Wow!

God gave Abraham a ram to take Isaac's place. And He gives us Jesus to take our place. We deserve to be punished for our sins. But God sent Jesus to die in our place!

Read verses 15-19

God mentioned His **three great promises** again.

1. Abraham would have loads of descendants (v17).

2. God would give them a land to live in (v17).

3. The whole world would be blessed through Abraham's descendants (v18). Number 3 is the most amazing promise...

Wow!

2000 years later, Jesus was born into Abraham's family. He died in our place to take the punishment for our sins. By doing this, Jesus was God's way of blessing the whole world. God kept His third promise by sending His own Son Jesus to die in our place!

Pray!

Anything you want to praise and thank God for?

Like father, like son

**1 John
4 v 10**

Abraham was willing to sacrifice his son Isaac for God.

But God provided a ram to take Isaac's place.

You might be wondering why God asked Abraham to sacrifice his son...

WEIRD WORDS

Atoning sacrifice
God punishes all sin. But He sent Jesus to take that punishment on the cross, in the place of everyone who trusts Him

One reason why God tested Abraham in this way was to give a picture of another Father who would sacrifice His own Son.

Any ideas who they were?

We'll find out in a minute. But first, here's a surprising fact...

The story of Abraham is in Genesis, the first book of the Old Testament. The Old Testament is the history of God's people, the Israelites. They're Abraham's descendants.

But that's not all. The Old Testament story also gives us pictures and clues about Jesus, who would come hundreds of years later.

And that's what this story of Abraham and Isaac does. It points us towards Jesus Christ.

**1. Abraham and Isaac
Read Genesis 22 v 2**
and fill in the missing vowels.

__br__h__m loved his son
Is__ __c so much, yet he was willing to s__cr__f__ce him for God.

**2. God and Jesus
Read 1 John 4 v 10**

G__d loved His Son J__s__s so much, yet He was w__ll__ng to s__cr__f__ce Him for us!

He sent Jesus to take the punishment we deserve for our sins! What an incredible gift God gave us!

Think & pray!

Have you accepted this gift? Have you turned to Jesus and asked Him to forgive you for all your sin? Spend time talking to God about your answer.

For the free e-booklet
Why did Jesus die?, email
discover@thegoodbook.co.uk
or check out
www.thegoodbook.co.uk/contact-us
to find our UK mailing address.

A tomb with a view

Genesis 23 v 1-20

We'll read a sad story today, but it shows just how much Abraham was trusting God to keep all of his promises...

WEIRD WORDS

Mourn
Show how upset he was

Hittites
The people who lived in the area

Choicest
Best

Intercede
Talk to him

400 shekels
4.6 kg of silver!

Merchants
Salesmen

Read Genesis 23 v 1-9

and fill in the missing words from the centre of the page.

> Sad news: S_____ died. She was _____ years old. Abraham wanted to bury her in C_____, the land God had promised him. He asked the H_____ to s_____ him a b_____ site. He specifically wanted to bury Sarah in a c_____ belonging to E_____.

Read verses 10-15

The Hittites and Ephron sound like they are talking about *gifts*, but it's really all about *buying and selling*.

> Ephron wanted to sell A_____ the whole f_____, not just the cave. This would cost much m_____. He charged Abraham _____ shekels of s_____, which seems very expensive.

(center word list, read top to bottom): cave Ephron field Hittites more price Sarah sell silver 400 127 Abraham agreed bought burial buried Canaan

Read verses 16-20

> Abraham a_____ to the p_____ and b_____ the burial plot from Ephron. He b_____ Sarah there.

Remember God's three great promises to Abraham? (See Day 66 for a reminder.) One of them was that God would give Abraham's family the whole land of Canaan.

So far, Abraham only owns a small plot of land in Canaan. But he buried Sarah in Canaan, trusting that one day God would give his family the whole land!

Pray!

Ask God to help you trust Him just as Abraham did.

Spot that wife!

**Genesis
24 v 1-16**

*Like yesterday,
today's missing
words can be
found in the
centre of the
page again.*

*But today they're
backwards.*

WEIRD WORDS

Canaanites
People living in
Canaan

Aram Naharaim
This area is now
called Iraq! It was
where Abraham's
family lived

Read Genesis 24 v 1-9

Abraham was o_____
and wanted his son
I_____ to marry a
good w_____. So he
sent his chief s_____
to find Isaac a wife. The
servant swore an o_____
with his h_____ under
Abraham's t_____.
He promised to find Isaac
a wife back in Abraham's
c_____.
He also promised not
to take Isaac away from
C_____. Abraham
trusted the L_____ to
I_____ his servant to a
wife for Isaac.

Abraham sent his servant 400
miles from Canaan to find a wife
for Isaac. But he wouldn't allow
Isaac to leave Canaan, because
Canaan was the land God had
promised to Abraham.

Read verses 10-16

Abraham's servant
travelled to A_____
N_____. He took
10 c_____ and loads
of good stuff to give to the
f_____ of Isaac's
future wife.

(centre word list, backwards)
gnirewsna daeL droL miarahaN slemac marA naanaC htao dlo yrtnuoc deyarp ylimaf hakebeR tnavres dnif dnah caasl ssendnik hgiht llew efiw

The servant hung out near
the w_____, hoping to
spot a wife for Isaac. He
p_____ for God
to show k_____
to Abraham and to
help him to f_____
Isaac a wife. While
he was still praying,
R_____ came to
the well. God was already
a_____
the servant's prayer!

Think!

God continued
to show kindness
to Abraham and to answer His
people's prayers.

How has God shown kindness to
you? How has He answered your
prayers?

_____
_____
_____
_____
_____
_____

Pray!

Thank God for the things you've
just written down. He's so faithful
to His people!

worshipped

She's the one

nose
marry
Nahor
praise
Rebekah

brother

**Genesis
24 v 17-54**

agreed

*Abraham sent
his servant 400
miles to find a
wife for Isaac.*

*The servant
asked God to
help him.*

*Maybe this girl
Rebekah is the
one for Isaac...*

*(Today's missing
words can be
found around
the page,
upside down.)*

bracelets

Read Genesis 24 v 17-25

R_____ gave the
servant some water from
her j_____. She even
fetched water for his ten
c_____! But he still
wasn't sure if she was the
one the L_____ had
chosen for I_____.
So he gave her a gold
n_____ ring and 2 gold
b_____. Then
he asked her about her
f_____. Rebekah
told him that she was the
granddaughter of N_____,
Abraham's b_____

family

camels

Now the servant knew that God had
answered his prayer. She was even
from the right family!

father

Read verses 26-27

The servant b_____
down and w_____
the Lord: "P_____
be to the Lord!"

WEIRD WORDS

Beka
About 6 grams

10 shekels
115 grams

Fodder
Animal food

Think!

God

bowed

How often do you praise
God and thank Him for
all He's given you? Sometimes we
don't even notice when God has
answered our prayers!

We'll skip verses 28-49. But here's
what happens in them.

• Rebekah's brother, Laban,
welcomed Abraham's servant into
their house.

Lord

• The servant told them all about
Abraham and how good God had
been to him.

• And all about the mission
Abraham had sent him on and
how God answered his prayer.

Next, read verses 50-54

Laban

L_____ and Bethuel
(Rebekah's f_____)
believed the servant. They
realised that G_____ was
behind it all and that He
was in control. So they
a_____ to let
Rebekah m_____ Isaac.

jar

God was in total control.
He showed His kindness to Abraham
yet again, He answered the servant's
prayer, and He was looking after
His people. Pleasingly, Laban and
Bethuel recognised this.

Isaac

Pray!

Thank God that He's in complete
control, and that He looks after
His people. Ask Him to help you
notice when He answers your
prayers.

Showing promise

**Genesis
24 v 54-67**

God has led
Abraham's
servant to
Rebekah.

She's the one God
wants Isaac to
marry.

Now it's time to
take her to meet
Isaac.

WEIRD WORDS

Detain me
Keep me here

The Negev
The desert

Meditate
Take time to focus
his thoughts on God

Read Genesis 24 v 54-60

Rebekah's family wanted her to stay
a little longer, but she decided it
was time to go and meet the man
she would marry.

*What did Rebekah's family say to
her (v60)? To find out, take **every
second letter** in the grid, starting
with the **first M**. When you get to
the end of the grid, start again from
the **first S**.*

M	S	A	C	Y	E	Y	N	O	D
U	A	B	N	E	T	C	S	O	C
M	O	E	N	T	Q	H	U	E	E
M	R	O	T	T	H	H	E	E	C
R	I	O	T	F	I	M	E	I	S
L	O	L	F	I	T	O	H	N	E
S	I	M	R	A	E	Y	N	Y	E
O	M	U	I	R	E	D	S	E	!

M＿ ＿   ＿ ＿ ＿

＿ ＿ ＿ ＿ ＿ ＿   ＿ ＿ ＿

＿ ＿ ＿ ＿ ＿ ＿   ＿ ＿

＿ ＿ ＿ ＿ ＿ ＿ ＿ ＿!

＿ ＿ ＿   ＿ ＿ ＿ ＿

＿ ＿ ＿ ＿ ＿ ＿ ＿ ＿ ＿ ＿ ＿

＿ ＿ ＿ ＿ ＿ ＿ ＿

＿ ＿ ＿   ＿ ＿ ＿ ＿ ＿ ＿

＿ ＿   ＿ ＿ ＿ ＿

＿ ＿ ＿ ＿ ＿ ＿!

They wanted her to have loads of
descendants. Well, she was about
to marry Isaac, Abraham's son.
Remember one of the promises God
made to Abraham?

*Find it in **Genesis 22 v 17** and put it
into your own words.*

God was keeping His promise to
Abraham. He and Isaac would have
loads of descendants!

They would become God's nation!

Read Genesis 24 v 61-67

Isaac married Rebekah. God was
keeping all of His promises!

Pray!

Thank you, Lord, that I can
trust you completely. Thank
you for keeping your promises
to Abraham. And especially for
blessing the whole world by
sending Jesus.

End of the road

Genesis 25 v 1-11

God found Isaac a loving wife — Rebekah. But what happened to Isaac's dad, Abraham?

WEIRD WORDS

Bore him
Gave birth to...

Concubines
Women belonging to Abraham

Gathered to his people
Joined his ancestors in death

Read Genesis 25 v 1-4

and unjumble the names of Abraham's sons.

Z_____
M A Z R I N

M_____
N E D M A

S_____
H U S H A

M_____
D I M I A N

J_____
K A N J O S H

I_____
S I K B A H

Read Genesis 25 v 5-6

> **Why did Isaac get so much more than Abraham's other sons?**

> **Isaac was the son God had promised to give Abraham. And it was through Isaac's family that God would keep His greatest promise...**

__ll p__ __pl__s on
__ __rth will be bl__ss__d
thr__ __gh y__ __
(Genesis 12 v 3)

Wow!

Jesus would be a descendant of Abraham and Isaac. God would bless people from every nation by sending Jesus to rescue them from sin!

Read Genesis 25 v 7-11

Abraham lived until he was 175! That fulfilled another one of God's promises to Abraham...

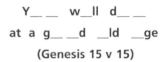

Y__ __ w__ll d__ __
at a g__ __d __ld __ge
(Genesis 15 v 15)

God had been so good to His servant Abraham. And even though Abraham was dead, God would continue to bless his family. And God's plan to bless the whole world would continue.

Pray!

Thank God for what He's taught you through Abraham's life story. Praise God that His perfect plans always work out.

*In the next issue of **Discover**: more from Genesis, Isaac, and God's plan to bless the world!*

Philippians: Joy for Jesus

When was your birthday? Can you remember what presents you got? And did you write any thank-you letters for them?

Thank-you letters can be boring, can't they? But today we're going to start looking at one of the best thank-you letters ever written! It's called **Philippians.**

PHILIPPIAN PHACT PHILE

- **Paul wrote this letter to Christians in Philippi (a city in northern Greece).**
- **Paul was a Christian who loved to tell people about Jesus.**
- **Paul wrote to thank the Philippians for a gift they'd sent him in prison.**
- **But he also wanted to encourage them to keep living for Jesus.**

Read Philippians 1 v 1-2

How did Paul describe himself and Timothy?

S_____ of

_____

They wanted to serve Jesus with everything they did. That meant living His way, telling people about Him and encouraging other Christians to serve Jesus.

Action!

Do YOU serve Jesus with your life? How can you serve Him more this week?

_____

_____

_____

Paul calls the Philippian Christians **"saints"** or **"holy people"** (depending on which Bible version you're reading). A saint is not just someone who was famous centuries ago. A saint is a person whose life is set aside to serve God. So if you're a Christian, you're a saint!

WEIRD WORDS

Timothy
Paul's close friend, who travelled with him, telling people about Jesus

Overseers and deacons
Church leaders

Grace and peace
A Christian greeting, praying that God will bless them

Pray!

1. Ask God to help you learn loads as you read Paul's letter to the Philippians.
2. Thank God that He wants you to serve Him!
3. Ask Him to help you serve Him in the ways you wrote down earlier.

God's great, Phils are brill

**Philippians
1 v 3-6**

*Surprisingly,
Paul doesn't
start his letter
by thanking
the Philippian
Christians for
their generous
gifts, but
by thanking
God for the
Philippians!*

WEIRD WORDS

The gospel

The great news
that Jesus can
rescue us from sin.
These Philippians
were partners in
the gospel because
they supported Paul
as he told people
about Jesus.

Read Philippians 1 v 3

What's the first thing Paul says?

Think!

Do you pray for other
Christians? Do you
thank God for what He's done for
them? Why not start today?

To download and print your own
Discover Prayer Diary,
email:
discover@thegoodbook.co.uk

Read verses 4-6

What does Paul thank God for (v5)?

That means they supported Paul as
he travelled around telling people
about Jesus.

Action!

How could you be
a gospel partner?
Maybe you could give pocket money
to missionaries or church.

Or you could make time to pray for
Christians you know who tell people
about Jesus.

What is Paul confident about? (v6)

That he who b__g__n this
g__ __d w__rk in you will
c__rry it on to completion
until the d__y of
Chr__st J__s__s

Wow!

God has started a good work in
every Christian, to make them more
like Jesus. And He'll finish the job on
the day when Jesus returns.

Pray!

On scrap paper, write down
names of Christians you could
pray for. Every day, try to pray for
2 or 3 of them. Thank God for
them and ask Him to use them in
great ways.

**Philippians
1 v 7-11**

*Paul is writing
to his friends in
Philippi.*

WEIRD WORDS

In chains
In prison

**Share in God's
grace**
They've all been
rescued from sin
by God

Depth of insight
Knowing the right
thing to do

Discern
Wisely decide

Blameless
Living God's way

**Fruit of
righteousness**
Things that show
you live God's way

Pray mates

Read Philippians 1 v 7-8

The friendship between Paul and the
Christians in Philippi was a special
one. There was something they all
loved, all worked for and all were
even prepared to suffer for.

What was it? Unjumble please!

> The g_____
> s p l o g e
> (v7)

It's one of the key words in this
letter. *Count how many times it
appears in chapter 1.*

The gospel is the great news that
Jesus can rescue people from sin.
The Philippians supported Paul as he
spread this good news. This really
deepened Paul's love for them.

Think!

Do you love Jesus?

Do you love other Christians? You
should, because they love Jesus too!

Read verses 9-11

*What three things did Paul pray for
them? Unjumble the anagrams to
find out.*

1. L_____ (v9)
    e v o l

Paul prayed that their love would
grow. Love for God and love for
other people.

2. K_____
    w o n k g l e e d

So that they could know the best
way to live (v9-10). That comes from
reading the Bible!

**3. That they would be
p_____ & b_____**
    repu   blessmale

Becoming more and more like Jesus,
showing some of His good qualities
(v10-11).

Pray!

Find the list of Christians you
made yesterday. Add any you
missed out. Choose at least 2 or
3 different people today. Spend
time praying for them. Pray the
3 things Paul prayed. And think
of specific stuff you can pray for
each of them.

Chained male

**Philippians
1 v 12-18**

*Paul had been
thrown into
prison for
telling people
about Jesus.*

*How do you
think he felt?*

_____

_____

_____

WEIRD WORDS

**Advance the
gospel**
Tell more people
about Jesus

Palace guard
Soldiers

Goodwill
The right reasons

False motives
Wrong reasons

Rejoice
Am happy

Read Philippians 1 v 12-13

Amazingly, Paul didn't see being
stuck in prison as a terrible thing,
but as a great opportunity.

*An opportunity for what?
Cross out all the Xs, Ys and Zs to
find out.*

Z	Z	Y	I	N	G	X	Y
X	Y	X	L	Z	P	Y	Z
T	E	L	Y	E	O	X
S	X	Z	Y	X	X	P	Z
U	Z	Y	Z	X	E	L	Y
S	E	J	T	Z	A	Z	X
Z	X	Y	U	O	B	Y	Z
X	Y	Z	X	Y	Z	X	Y

T_ _ _ _ _ _

_ _ _ _ _ _ _

_ _ _ _ _

_ _ _

Paul got the chance to talk about
Jesus with the prison guards! And
that's not all…

Read verses 14-18

Despite being locked up, Paul still
told loads of people about Jesus!
This encouraged many other
Christians to be brave and talk
about Jesus too! Some of them
didn't like Paul and did it for the
wrong reasons (v15), but they were
still teaching the truth about Jesus!

Wow!

In some parts of the
world, Christians are
hassled, imprisoned, beaten or
even killed for talking about Jesus.
It makes any teasing we get seem
easy! We should be much braver in
telling people about Jesus. What's
the worst that can happen?!

Pray!

Thank God for Christians who
suffer for the gospel.
Ask God to give you the courage
and opportunities to tell your
friends and family about Jesus.

For the free fact sheet
*How to tell your friends about
Jesus*, email
discover@thegoodbook.co.uk
or check out
www.thegoodbook.co.uk/
contact-us to find our UK mailing
address.

Life or death

**Philippians
1 v 19-26**

*Paul is writing
to the Philippian
Christians from
prison. But he
doesn't seem too
down about it!*

WEIRD WORDS

**Spirit of Jesus
Christ**
Holy Spirit

Deliverance
Rescue. Either
from prison, or by
death so that he
goes to heaven!

Exalted
Given honour and
praise because of
the way Paul lived
for Jesus

Fruitful labour
Successful work,
telling people
about Jesus

Boasting
Saying how great
Jesus is!

Read Philippians 1 v 19-20

Paul knows that God will look after
him and things will work out for the
best.

*How can he be so confident?
Go back one letter to find out
(B=A, C=B, D=C etc).*

1. __ __ __ __ __ __
   Q S B Z F S

Lots of people were praying for him.
Paul knew that God would answer
their prayers and that God's plans
for him would work out.

2. __ __ __ __ __ __
   T Q J S J U

__ __ __ __ __ __ __
P G K F T V T

Paul had the Holy Spirit with him.
When Jesus went back to heaven,
He gave His Spirit to live in the lives
of all Christians. The Spirit helps us
to live God's way.

Here's an easy question for you:

LIFE or DEATH?

Which would you choose?

Read verses 21-26

> ## Life
> If he stayed alive, he would be able
> to tell more people about Jesus.
> And he would be able to teach and
> encourage other Christians.

> ## Death
> If Paul was sentenced to death,
> then he would go to be with Jesus
> in heaven. Paul couldn't imagine
> anything better than that!

__ __   __ __ __ __
U P   M J W F

__ __   __ __ __ __ __ __
J T   D I S J T U

__ __ __   __ __   __ __ __
B O E   U P   E J F

__ __   __ __ __ __ **(v21)**
J T   H B J O

The main point of living is to serve
Jesus Christ. Yet by dying, Christians
gain being with Jesus. Both life
and death should have Jesus at the
centre!

Think & pray!

Read verse 21 again.
Can you honestly say that?
Ask God to help you to become
like that, so that Jesus is the most
important person in your life.

78

Philippians
1 v 27-30

Paul was in prison and might even be put to death.

But he was still happy and excited about serving God!

WEIRD WORDS

Striving together
Standing up for Jesus

Grand stand

What about the Philippian Christians? Life was tough for them too!

PHILIPPIAN PHACT PHILE

- **The city of Philippi belonged to the Romans.**
- **Christians there would have been hassled because of their faith.**
- **False teachers got at them too, telling them lies.**
- **They also had to stand up against all the wrong things people did.**

Read Philippians 1 v 27

Paul is saying…

> **Live godly lives for God. Stick together and support each other. And stand up for the truth about Jesus.**

Think!

What do you need to change so that you live in a way that pleases God more?

_____

_____

_____

Action!

How can you get closer to and support other Christians?

_____

_____

_____

Read verses 28-30

Do you ever think that being a Christian is the soft option?

That it's only for weedy nerds?

Think again! The Christian life is **tough**. Christians are involved in a battle against sin, and this often makes people laugh at them or hate them.

Pray!

It's a privilege to stand up for our belief in Jesus and even to suffer for Him!
Ask God to give you the desire and courage to make a stand for Him and not back down.

Man (& woman) United

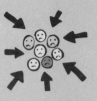

*The church in
Philippi are being
threatened by
people who are
against them and
hate Jesus.*

*What can they
do???*

WEIRD WORDS

**Common sharing
in the Spirit**
Living God's way
with the Holy Spirit's
help

**Tenderness and
compassion**
Loving kindness

Vain conceit
Pride. Thinking
you're better than
other people

Also, arguments, selfishness and
pride were starting to crop up
among the Christians.

*(By the way, all of today's missing
words are in the wordsearch.)*

C	T	O	G	E	T	H	E	R
B	O	B	A	C	O	J	N	P
E	T	M	Q	L	O	V	E	U
T	H	X	F	Z	C	P	M	R
T	E	M	G	O	H	T	I	P
E	R	Y	D	S	R	U	N	O
R	S	P	I	R	I	T	D	S
S	E	L	F	I	S	H	E	E
F	H	U	N	I	T	E	D	D

Read Philippians 2 v 1-2

Paul reminded them that

they were u_____ with

C_____. Jesus' love

c_____ them.

They were living God's way

with the S_____'s

help.

All of that means that Christians
have a close relationship with Jesus.
He loves them, and His Spirit is with
them, helping them to serve Him!

*So what advice did Paul give to help
them to serve Jesus more?*

Read verses 2-4

1. Be like-minded.

Serve Jesus t_____r!

Have the same l_____ and

be of the same m_____.

That means you too! Get together
with other Christians. Talk and pray
together. Work out ways you can
serve God together.

2. Put others first!

Do nothing out of

s_____ ambition

or to make yourself look

good. Consider others

b_____ than yourselves.

Don't just look after your

own interests but also the

interests of o_____.

Think & pray!

How can you put others first?

_____

_____

Ask God to help you get on
better with other Christians. Ask
Him to help you care more for
them and put them first.

80

**Philippians
2 v 5-8**

Down to earth

Jesus gave up heaven to come to earth, to rescue you and me! Maybe you've never really thought about what actually happened. *Have you truly appreciated the amazing love Jesus showed?*

Today Paul reminds us…

Read Philippians 2 v 5-8

How long ago was Christmas? Weeks? Months? Nearly a year?! Are all the food, decorations and gifts a fading memory?

What about the Christmas story — Jesus' story? Is that a fading memory too?

Jesus in heaven
Living in total peace with His Father
Enjoying the perfect happiness of heaven
Being in charge of the whole universe

But Jesus left all that behind, humbled Himself, and came down to earth!

Now fill in the missing verse numbers please.

WEIRD WORDS

Human likeness
Jesus became a human being, like you and me

Humbled himself
God's Son became a servant!

Jesus on earth
Became a man Verse _____ Born as a human baby Had no proper home Hated by people
Became a servant Verse _____ Did everything God sent Him to do Healed the sick Forgave people's sins
Was willing to die Verse _____ He suffered a horrible death on the cross. He did it for you and me, to rescue us from sin.

Incredible! Jesus was the perfect example of being humble, loving, and serving others. We need to give up our selfishness and pride to become more like Jesus (v5).

Pray!

Thank Jesus for giving up everything in heaven to come to earth to die in our place. Ask God to help you to become more like Jesus.

Wow! Bow now!

81

Philippians 2 v 9-11

Recap time.

God wants us to live for Him, support each other and be humble and loving.

Why?

Because Jesus gave up everything to die for us.

WEIRD WORDS

Exalted him
Put Jesus in a high and important position where He'll get all the praise and glory

---

Jesus gave up so much for us.

*Look back at yesterday's Discover page to find three things Jesus gave up (they're under "**Jesus in heaven**").*

Jesus gave up...

1. _____
_____

2. _____
_____

3. _____
_____

That's why God gives Jesus the highest honour.

Read Philippians 2 v 9-11

Jesus has been given the highest position so that…

(rearrange the word blocks)

At		

Jesus		name
	At	
every	the	knee
	of	bow
should		

That means that one day everyone will **worship** Jesus.

Wow!

People who truly bow down and worship Jesus are those who really believe that He is God, in charge of their lives. Worshipping Jesus means living your life His way. Loving Him, serving Him, telling people about Him. Will you do that?

Pray!

Today's verses are in an old song…
*At the name of Jesus
Every knee shall bow,
Every tongue confess Him,
King of glory now.
He is God the Saviour,
He is Christ the Lord,
Ever to be worshipped,
Trusted and adored.*

Use these words to praise Jesus right now.

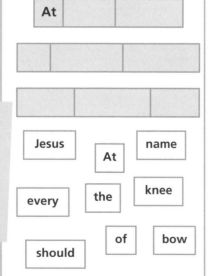

Mark: Who is Jesus?

**Mark
9 v 30-35**

Let's head back to Mark's book about Jesus.

The disciples are still confused...

Peter had worked out that Jesus was the **Christ/Messiah** — the King who'd come to rescue God's people. But the disciples still didn't fully understand what Jesus had come to do.

Read Mark 9 v 30-32

and fill in the gaps.

The S_____ of Man will be handed over to men who will k_____ him. And after t_____ days he will r_____.

Jesus told His disciples that He would die and then be raised back to life! Jesus came to earth specifically to do those things. But the disciples didn't get it.

Read verses 33-35

We beat Eastside 5-0 and I scored 2 great goals!

Er, that's great. But did I ever tell you about the time I scored a hat trick?

Ever boast about stuff? Or try to prove that you're a bit better than someone else? That's what the disciples were doing. *But what did Jesus tell them?*

If anyone wants to be f_____, they must be l_____, and the s_____ of all.

Stop putting yourself first!

Action!

So how will you put that into practice this week?

- ☐ **Try to cut out boasting**
- ☐ **Compliment mates when they do something good**
- ☐ **Offer to wash up for a week**
- ☐ **Give a gift to someone who's ill or fed up**
- ☐ **Keep your room clean**
- ☐ **Be nicer to your bro or sis**
- ☐ _____
- ☐ _____

Pray!

Now ask God to help you!

More about serving tomorrow...

WEIRD WORDS

Son of Man
Jesus — as well as being God's Son, He was a human being

The Twelve
Jesus' 12 disciples

**Mark
9 v 36-41**

Have you done any of the serving suggestions from yesterday?

Today Jesus gives us three top tips for serving people and putting others first.

Serving suggestions

Read Mark 9 v 36-37

Cross out the Xs!

XXWHOXEXVERXWEXX
LCOMEXSOXNEOFXXTH
XEXSECHIXLDXXREXN
IXNMXYNAXMEXXWEX
LCOMEXXSMEXX

W_____

_____

_____

_____

Back then, kids were considered unimportant. They had no rights and not much education.

Top tip 1
We should be welcoming to people, especially those worse off than us. It's like welcoming Jesus Himself!

☐ I will be more friendly towards

_____

(the name of an elderly person, or kid at school).

Read verses 38-40

John thought that only the twelve disciples could follow Jesus and serve God. Jesus told him not to be so narrow-minded!

Top tip 2
Don't think you're better than other Christians. If they're serving God too, then show them support!

☐ I'll be more supportive to

_____ even though we disagree about stuff.

Read verse 41

Even giving a drink to another Christian pleases Jesus!

Top tip 3
Christians should help each other out. It pleases Jesus!

☐ I can _____

_____ to help out

_____

Action!

Hopefully you've decided to do loads of good serving stuff. To remind you to do it all, turn these things into a poster and stick it up. And ask God to give you a helping hand.

WEIRD WORDS

Demons
Evil spirits that live in people, causing them to be ill or do sinful stuff

**Mark
9 v 42-50**

Sin is when we do what WE want instead of what GOD wants.

Jesus used brilliant picture language to show us how serious sin is.

Draw pictures to complete the sentences.

WEIRD WORDS

Millstone
Really heavy stone slab used to crush wheat

Maimed
Disabled

Quenched
Put out

Chop it off!

Read Mark 9 v 42

It would be better to be thrown into the → [ ] with a [ ] around your neck than to cause a young Christian to sin.

Ordinary Christians are precious to Jesus. He loves it when people get to know Him. And anyone who causes them to sin is in serious trouble!

Read verses 43-48

If your [ ] causes you to sin, cut it off! And if your [ ] causes you to sin, cut that off too! And pluck out your [ ] if it causes you to sin. It's better to lose a hand, foot or eye than to be thrown into hell!

Jesus doesn't mean we should actually chop off body bits if we sin! He's pointing out how deadly serious sin is. People who refuse to turn away from sinning against God will be thrown into hell.

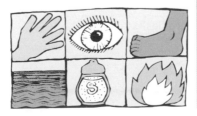

Action!

We must cut out the stuff that causes us to sin. If it's stuff on TV, stop watching it! If it's stuff we read or listen to, throw it away! If it's how we use social media, stop using it! If it's certain friends, then we must stop hanging out with them. Obvious, really!

Read verses 49-50

Everyone will be salted/purified by → [ ]

Weird phrase! This probably means that all Christians can expect to be persecuted for following Jesus.

[ ] is good unless it loses its saltiness

Christians should be salty! They should be tasty! That means they should stand out from the crowd and not just live like everyone else. **Jesus** should shine through their lives. And they should not fall out with each other!

Pray!

What have you learned today? What do you need to sort out?

_____

_____

Talk to God about it.

The D-word

Mark 10 v 1-12

Divorce.

It's a tricky subject.

It causes a lot of pain and upset.

But the Pharisees used it to try and trick Jesus...

WEIRD WORDS

Judea
Area around Jerusalem

Pharisees
Ultra-strict Jewish people

Adultery
Cheating on your husband or wife

Read Mark 10 v 1-2

Jesus was in the area where Herod Antipas ruled. John the Baptist had been arrested for speaking against Herod's divorce and remarriage. The Pharisees wanted Jesus to get arrested too.

Read verses 3-5

Moses allowed couples to get divorced only because so many people were sinning in their marriages. It was a last resort if the situation was terrible. But many people were using Moses' law as an excuse for an easy divorce. Shocking.

Read verses 6-9

Use the word square to show what God's plan for marriage was.

female	father	God
joined	male	man	mother
one	separate	wife

G_____ created humans to be m_____ and f_____. A m_____ will leave his f_____ and m_____ to marry his w_____. The two will become o_____ flesh. So, what God has j_____, let no one s_____.

This is God's plan for marriage. A husband and wife are joined together and should never be separated.

Read verses 10-12

Marriage should be for life. That is God's plan. Sadly, it doesn't always work out that way. People do get divorced and families are split up. Going against God's plan causes masses of hurt.

Pray!

for people you know who are suffering because of divorce or family break-up. Ask God to be at the centre of their lives.

Pray!

for married couples you know — that they'll never want to give up.

Have YOU suffered a family break-up? Do you have questions about divorce or family issues? If so, email discover@thegoodbook.co.uk or check out www.thegoodbook.co.uk/contact-us to find our UK mailing address.

**Mark
10 v 13-16**

Oi!
Clear off!

*Ever felt
unwanted?*

*The kids in
today's Bible
bit did...*

Pesky kids!

Read Mark 10 v 13-14

Jesus was furious with His disciples for turning the kids away. *Crack the Morse code to reveal what He said.*

```
_ _ _ _ ' _ _ _ _ _
-••/---/-•/-/•••/-/---/•--•
```

```
_ _ _ _ '   _ _ _ _
-/••••/•/--/   -/••••/•
```

```
_ _ _ _ _ _ _ _ _ _
-•/••/-•/-•/-••/---/--
```

```
_ _ _ _   _ _ _ _
---/••-•/  --•/---/-••
```

```
_ _ _ _ _ _ _ _ _
-•••/•/•-••/---/-•/--•/••
```

```
_ _   _ _ _ _ _
-/---/  •••/••-/-•-•/••••
```

```
_ _ _   _ _ _ _ _ _
•-/•••/  -/••••/•/•••/•
```

A	•—
B	—•••
C	—•—•
D	—••
E	•
F	••—•
G	——•
H	••••
I	••
J	•———
K	—•—
L	•—••
M	——
N	—•
O	———
P	•——•
Q	——•—
R	•—•
S	•••
T	—
U	••—
V	•••—
W	•——
X	—••—
Y	—•——
Z	——••

```
•—/—•/—•——/———/—•/•
```

```
_   _ _ _ _ _
•——/••••/———/   •——/———/—•/—
```

```
_ _ _ _ _ _ _ _
•—•/•/—•—•/•/••/••—/•••—/•
```

```
_
—/••••/•
```

```
_ _ _ _ _ _ _
—•/••/—•—•/—••/—••/———/—
```

```
_ _ _ _ _ _
———/••—•/  ——•/———/—••
```

```
_ _ _ _ _
•—••/••/—•/•/  •—
```

```
_ _ _ _ '
—•—/•••/••/•—••/—••/•—/———/—•/
```

```
_ _ _   _
•/—•/  /•/• •/  ••/—
```

Wow!

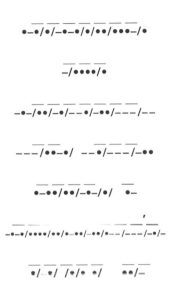

Kids are important to Jesus. We shouldn't just treat them as a nuisance. We should spend time with them, and talk to them about Jesus.

Think!

How can you follow Jesus' example? Spend more time with your younger bro' or sis'? Volunteer to help out at Sunday School or Kids' Club?

Read verses 15-16

Wow!

The kingdom of God means having your life ruled by God. And one day going to live with Him for ever! We can only be part of God's kingdom if we depend on God like little kids depend on their parents! Trusting Him for everything and letting Him have control of our lives.

Pray!

If you want to join God's kingdom, tell Him that you're sorry for disobeying Him. Tell Him you depend on Him completely. Ask Him to forgive your sins and take control of your life.

WEIRD WORDS

Rebuked them
Told them off

Indignant
Angry at something that's unfair

Hinder
Stop

Blessed
Prayed for

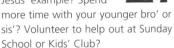

Dash for cash

*Ready to hear
what Jesus has
to say today?*

It'll cost you...

*(By the way,
today's answers
are all in the
wordsearch.)*

```
C L F M N G A J E S U S
B O O E T E R N A L Q A
R O M S R L U E S O T D
Q K F M E G L P Y V D E
U E P Y A H E A V E N Z
G D E M S N O D U D S J
B O Y Z U O D Q A R W V
R H M N R T C M C J E K
D K N E E S H A E O A L
O A V X V E F N K N L P
O L D N T L H C B J T K
G O D W X L R O O P H S
```

I go to church
and live a
good life...

Read Mark 10 v 17

A m_____ ran up to
J_____ and fell on his
k_____. *"What must I do
to receive e_____
life?"* he asked.

*Are you running towards Jesus or
away from Him? Are you interested
in eternal life?*

Read verses 18-20

**Jesus told the guy that
no one is g_____
except G_____. Then Jesus
asked him if he knew the
c_____.
*"I have kept a_____ of them
since I was a b_____,"* said
the man.**

The guy thought he'd been good
enough to deserve eternal life! But
Jesus had just told him that no one
is truly good except God.

Wow!

None of us is good enough
to gain eternal life. We've all
sinned and sin stops us from
being good enough. We can't earn
eternal life by living a good life. Only
Jesus can give it to us, if we turn to
Him and have our sins forgiven.

Read verses 21-22

**Jesus l_____ at
him and l_____ him.
He said, *"Go and s_____
everything you have and
give to the p_____. Then
you'll have t_____
in h_____."* The man
went away s_____ because
he had great w_____.**

He thought he'd been good enough
to **earn** eternal life. But money was
more important to him than God was.

Think!

Jesus knows what is in our hearts.
What's the most important thing
in your life?

_____

Will you follow Jesus or will you
walk away? Your choice...

WEIRD WORDS

Eternal life
Everlasting life!
With God!

**Give false
testimony**
Lie

**Mark
10 v 23-27**

Yesterday we read the sad story about a rich guy who chose money instead of eternal life with God.

Got the hump?

What would you do to earn a million?

☐ **Eat your own weight in bananas**

☐ **Sit in a bath of live worms**

☐ **Wear your mum's clothes for a week**

☐ **Run down the street naked**

Many people think that money is the answer to all their problems. But Jesus says that having stacks of cash counts for nothing.

**Read Mark 10 v 23-25
Jesus reckons it's easier for...**

to get through here

than for

to get into God's kingdom!

Sadly, money can take over people's lives. It becomes much more important to them than God. Just like the guy we read about yesterday.

Read verse 26

The disciples were baffled.

Rearrange these words to form their question.

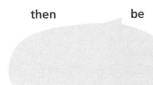

then   be   Who   saved?   can

Check out Jesus' amazing answer in verse 27

EVERYBODY CAN BE SAVED!
Because God can do what is totally impossible for us puny people. Nothing we can do can save us and give us eternal life with Jesus.

But God can save us!

Pray!

If you've already asked God to save you from sin, then you've got LOADS to thank Him for. If you haven't, maybe now is a good time...

**Mark
10 v 28-34**

Jesus told a rich guy that he had to give up his money if he wanted eternal life.

God had to come first in his life.

WEIRD WORDS

The gospel
The good news about Jesus

Persecutions
Getting hassled for being a Christian

Gentiles
Non-Jewish people. Here, it means the Romans

Flog him
Whip him

Give it up

Peter had something to say…

Read Mark 10 v 28

> We have left
> e_____
> to follow you!

The disciples had left their jobs, homes and families to follow Jesus.

Wow!

Being a follower of Jesus Christ (a Christian) can be costly. Sometimes we'll lose friends or our families will turn against us. We also have to turn away from things that used to be more important to us than Jesus.

Read verses 29-31

Top news! If we give up things or if we suffer for following Jesus, God will look after us!

And one day we'll get to live with Him!

What else did Jesus say?

> Many who are f_____
> will be l_____, and the
> l_____ will be f_____

Things will be very different. Christians who were poor or persecuted on earth will be rewarded in eternal life!

Read verses 32-34

> We're going to J_____, where the Son of M_____ will be handed over to the chief p_____. They will sentence him to d_____ and hand him over to the G_____, who will m_____ him, s_____ on him, flog him and k_____ him. Three days later, he will r_____.

Read through that again.

That's what Jesus would go through for His followers. He would be betrayed. He would suffer and die. But He would be raised back to life to beat sin and death for ever!

*So, are **you** prepared to stick your neck out for Him? To put Jesus first in your life?*

Pray!

Dear Jesus, thank you so much for what you went through for me. Please help me to give up stuff that gets in the way of serving you. Give me the strength to cope when I'm hassled for following you.

Chasing fame

Want to be famous?

People would give you respect and tell you how great you are!

James and John wanted fame and power...

WEIRD WORDS

Indignant
Angry

Gentiles
Non-Jewish people

Exercise authority
Boss them around

Read Mark 10 v 35-37

James and John knew that Jesus was the Christ — God's chosen King. Maybe they imagined Him sitting on a throne...

What did they ask Jesus (v37)?

They wanted to be great and powerful.

Read verses 38-40

What is Jesus talking about?

Jesus talks about *"drinking the cup"* He drinks and *"being baptised"* like Him. Jesus is talking about His death! It's the cup full of God's anger that He *"drank"* for us when He died on the cross. He took God's punishment for our sins.

James and John probably didn't want that kind of greatness! Following Jesus will mean suffering for Him.

Read verses 41-44

Jesus talked about Roman rulers who bossed people around.

Jesus says His followers shouldn't chase praise and popularity. We should *serve* others!

Action!

Flick back to Days 82 and 83. What things did you say you'd do to serve people?

_____

_____

_____

How's it going? Well done if you've done some of them!
If not, you'd best start now!

Pray!

Say sorry to God for the times you chase after praise and popularity. Ask God to help you serve people by doing the things you wrote down.

The Servant King

Mark 10 v 45

> If one of you wants to be great, he must be servant of the rest.

Jesus is God's Son — the Creator and Ruler of the whole universe. What would He know about being a servant???

Quite a lot actually.

Read Mark 10 v 45

Use the code to discover what Jesus said.

[coded puzzle]

Jesus is the **Christ/Messiah**, God's chosen King. He's in charge of everything. He's awesome!

But He came as a **servant**! He loves us so much that He came to **rescue** us from our sin.

Why do we need rescuing?

Sin gets in the way between us and God. It stops us from knowing Him and being His friends. The final result of sin is **death**. That's why we need rescuing!

How did Jesus rescue us?

As you know, Jesus was cruelly nailed to a cross and left to die. As He died, all of our **sin** (the wrong stuff we've done) was put onto Jesus. He took the **punishment** we deserve!

A **ransom** is money paid to set people free. Jesus died in our place, as our ransom — buying our freedom. **Jesus gave up his life to pay the price for our sins!** This means we can turn to Jesus and ask Him to **forgive** all our sins!

For the free fact sheet

How to Become a Christian, email discover@thegoodbook.co.uk or check out www.thegoodbook.co.uk/contact-us to find our UK mailing address.

WEIRD WORDS

Son of Man
Jesus Christ

Ransom
Price paid to set people free

A B C D E F G H I L M N O R S T U V Y

**Mark
10 v 46-52**

*Jesus and His
disciples are
on their way
to Jerusalem,
where Jesus will
die.*

*Today they stop
off in Jericho.*

WEIRD WORDS

Jericho
City 15 miles from
Jerusalem

Son of David
Jesus was a
descendant of King
David

Have mercy
Show kindness

Rebuked
Criticised

Rabbi
Teacher

Blind faith

Read Mark 10 v 46-52

*Fill in the missing words and then fit
them into the crossword.*

**Bartimaeus was a
(1) b _ _ _ _ man who
was (2) b _ _ _ _ _ _ by
the side of the road. When
he saw Jesus, he shouted,
*Son of (3) D _ _ _ _, have
mercy on me!"* People tried
to shut him up, but
(4) J _ _ _ _ said,
*"What do you want me to
do?" "I want to (5) s _ _."*
So Jesus (6)h _ _ _ _ _
Bartimaeus and he
(7) f _ _ _ _ _ _ _
Jesus along the road.**

Bartimaeus called Jesus **Son of
David**. That's a name used in
the Old Testament for the Christ/
Messiah — the King who would
rescue God's people. Bartimaeus
believed that Jesus was this King.

Because he **believed** in Jesus,
Jesus healed him. Then Bartimaeus
followed Jesus.

What about you?

Think & pray!

Do you believe that Jesus died for
you? Do you follow Him?
If you do, thank God for giving
you the faith to do so.
If you're not sure, ask God to help
you to believe, and to learn more
about Jesus as you read the Bible.

**Want to know more about
following Jesus?**
Email
discover@thegoodbook.co.uk
or check out
www.thegoodbook.co.uk/contact-us
to find our UK mailing address.

More from Mark next issue...

DISCOVER
COLLECTION

ISSUE 3

DISCOVER ISSUE 3

Meet Jacob the Schemer in Genesis. Listen to great teaching from Jesus, in Mark. Find out how the first Christians get on in Acts. And let Philippians challenge you to really live for Jesus every day.

DISCOVER

BIBLE NOTES FOR YOUNG PEOPLE

THREE MONTHS OF EXPLORING GOD'S WORD:
* **Jesus:** The ultimate hero
* **Jacob:** Changed cheat
* **Acts:** Spreading the news
* **Philippians:** Living for Jesus

ISSUE 3

COLLECT 12 THE SET

COLLECT ALL 12 ISSUES TO COMPLETE THE DISCOVER COLLECTION

Don't forget to order the next issue of Discover. Or even better, grab a one-year subscription to make sure Discover lands in your hands as soon as it's out. Packed full of puzzles, prayers and pondering points.

DISCOVER

thegoodbook.co.uk   thegoodbook.com

thegoodbook
COMPANY